THE
ELEGANT
CHEF'S GUIDE TO
HORS D'OEUVRES
AND APPETIZERS

THE ELEGANT CHEF'S GUIDE TO HORS D'OEUVRES AND APPETIZERS

ANTONY
WORRALL–THOMPSON

Photographs by Bryce Attwell

CHARTWELL
BOOKS, INC.

To all the young ladies in my past and to MILIIZA-JANE, my present and future ....

Text © Antony Worrall-Thompson 1984
Photographs © Bryce Attwell 1984

Editor Jane Lunzer
Designed by Sara Komar

Published by Chartwell Books, Inc.
A division of Book Sales, Inc.
110 Enterprise Avenue
Secaucus, New Jersey 07094
By arrangement with
George Weidenfeld & Nicolson Limited
91 Clapham High Street, London sw4 7TA

ISBN 0-89009-774-7

Filmset in Great Britain by Keyspools Limited, Golborne, Lancashire
Colour separations by Newsele Litho Limited, Milan
Printed and bound in Italy by L.E.G.O., Vicenza

CONTENTS

INTRODUCTION

In November 1981 I created a stir among the conventional London restaurant world by opening the Ménage à Trois, a restaurant serving only appetizers and desserts. Most people dismissed it as a passing gimmick, but three years have now passed and not only is the restaurant still open but it is an unqualified success.

The idea came to me as a result of dining on many occasions with various ladies who, almost without exception, would say 'I wish I could just have a couple of appetizers'. Invariably the waiter would make it clear that this was unacceptable. There was clearly an opportunity to be taken if it could be tackled in the right way. I determined to create exciting dishes based on two important principles: the produce must be of the highest standards and the finished dishes must be appealing to the eye as well as to the palate – principles to which all good cooks must adhere.

From eating in many of the best restaurants I had noticed that, although the food was excellent, very few people seemed to be relaxed. I questioned the possible reasons: was it the décor? I decided to have pretty, feminine surroundings; was it the lack of music? I introduced a pianist to promote a relaxed, club-like atmosphere; was there something in the attitude of the waiters that unnerved customers? I employed attractive and intelligent young women who made the customers feel welcome. I felt too that the stuffiness of traditional wine lists could be intimidating, so with the help of my friend and head barman, Eddie Khoo, we introduced amazing cocktails and a large variety of moderately-priced wines. Having flouted the conventions of established dining to such an extent I decided that in some areas I should adopt a traditional approach and carry it out with impeccable attention to detail: crisp white table linen, beautiful flowers, delicate glassware and sparkling silver. The result has been a restaurant full of cheerful people and, even more gratifying, a place where women happily entertain one another.

This book contains recipes for many of the most successful and exciting dishes we have created for the restaurant. Use them and the accompanying photographs to fire your imagination. Have fun experimenting with different combinations: as your confidence grows, so will your cooking ability.

Finally, there are several people who deserve my thanks: Donald and Annie Foster Firth helped me set up Ménage à Trois; Jane Lunzer has been a tower of strength and patience in helping me put this book together; Bryce Attwell's photographs have magnificently captured the appearance of the dishes; the cookbooks of Elizabeth David, Jane Grigson, Michel Guérard and Fredy Giradet continually inspire me to better things; Michel and Albert Roux are great chefs who have strived to introduce new produce into this country – without their efforts restaurants in Great Britain would still be years behind those in France; David Wilby and Frank Rourke, chefs at Ménage à Trois, have maintained a high standard of cooking during my frequent absences while writing this book; and finally my wife, Militza-Jane, who suffered numerous trials and tribulations as I tested the recipes at home.

HOW TO USE THIS BOOK

* Quantities for the recipes in this book (when given) are intended as first courses, serving four people. To serve more people, increase all the ingredients proportionately. If, however, you wish to serve the dishes as substantial main courses, only increase the quantity of the main ingredients – the meat, fish or vegetable. Ingredients for sauces and presentation remain the same.

* Look up ingredients in the notes, *pages 149–55*: there may be a substitute for an ingredient you find hard to purchase or too expensive. (Rare produce can be found in ethnic shops and markets – Greek, Oriental, Middle Eastern – delicatessens, gourmet shops and the international section of large supermarkets.) The notes will also give approximate times for blanching vegetables and other useful information.

* Read the list of ingredients and method for the recipe carefully: you will notice that almost all the ingredients require some preparation before assembling the dish. This should be done *earlier in the day*: such work includes making stocks, blanching vegetables, making pie dough, boning and trimming meat and fish. Recipes for sauces, dressings, etc., are given at the end of the book, with a page reference given in the main recipe which refers to them.

* This is essentially a cooking of speed; if advance preparation of ingredients has been carried out, most dishes should not take longer than 15 to 20 minutes to complete (apart from soups and cold mousses).

* Half an hour before serving the dish, make the sauce and keep it warm in a bain-marie. Dot the surface with butter or cover it with buttered wax paper to stop a skin forming.

* Times given are approximations. Who am I to tell you how you should cook your meat, fish or vegetables? I know how I like them cooked, but this may not be to your taste.

* Temperatures given are also merely a guide. I cannot judge the efficiency or correctness of your oven or burners; therefore I specify only low ($275°–325°$F), medium ($350°–375°$F) or hot ($400°–450°$F).

* Use the photograph of each dish as another guide; it can be frustrating to read wonderful recipes that inspire you, only to be daunted by not knowing how to present them.

* This is above all 'spontaneous cooking': treat the recipes as suggestions to trigger off inspiration. Substitute sauces and garnishes, experiment with new combinations. May I mention, however, that if at all possible you should decorate your creations only with edible ingredients, avoiding the conventional and unappetizing tomato 'roses' and shellfish heads. Try to make all the items on the plate complement each other.

Basket of Crudités
with homemade Dips

MAIN INGREDIENTS

raw vegetables carrots, cauliflower florets, young artichokes, white Oriental radishes, Jerusalem artichokes, avocado, red cabbage, celery, celery root, Belgian endive, cucumber, fennel, kohlrabi, button mushrooms, scallions, peppers, radishes, sea kale, tomatoes, small turnips

blanched vegetables young green beans, broccoli florets, zucchini, small leeks, snow peas, new potatoes, asparagus, oyster plant
quail's eggs, hard-boiled
gull's eggs, hard-boiled

The selection of vegetables does not need to be wide. Arrange them on lettuce or other salad leaves in a basket or dish and serve with one or both of the following cold dips:

ANCHOVY DIP

$\frac{3}{4}$ c olive oil
1 small can anchovies
3 cloves garlic, crushed
$\frac{1}{2}$ tsp fresh thyme leaves
$\frac{1}{2}$ tsp chopped fresh ginger
$\frac{1}{2}$ tsp fresh chopped basil
1 Tbsp Dijon mustard
1 Tbsp lemon juice
1 egg
2 tsp capers
$\frac{1}{2}$ tsp granulated sugar
$\frac{1}{2}$ tsp black pepper

ROUILLE

$\frac{3}{4}$ c olive oil
3 hard-boiled egg yolks
2 raw egg yolks
3 cloves garlic, finely chopped
1 tsp tomato purée
$\frac{1}{2}$ tsp ground ginger
juice of 1 lemon
pinch of saffron stamen, soaked in
   1 Tbsp warm water
$1\frac{1}{2}$ tsp Dijon mustard
$\frac{1}{2}$ tsp cayenne pepper
salt and white pepper

For each dip, combine all the ingredients except the oil in a food processor or blender. Process until smooth. With the machine running, add oil in a continuous trickle until the sauce emulsifies.

A colorful and convenient way of serving a large number of people with something more refreshing than potato chips or peanuts.

Iced Tomato Bisque with Avocado and Basil Sherbet

MAIN INGREDIENTS

4 slices stale white bread, crusts
  removed
1 Tbsp red wine vinegar
4 cloves garlic, chopped
1 Tbsp granulated sugar
6 Tbsp olive oil
1½lb tomatoes, peeled and seeded
1 pt tomato juice
6 scallions, finely chopped
1 medium-sized cucumber, peeled
  and chopped
2 sweet red bell peppers, peeled,
  seeded and chopped
2 Tbsp fresh chopped basil
ice cubes
salt and white pepper

PRESENTATION

4 scoops avocado and basil sherbet,
  page 140
12 fresh basil leaves

---

1 Crumble the bread and place in a blender or food processor. Add the vinegar and blend, then the garlic and sugar and blend once again.

---

2 With the blender running slowly, add as much olive oil as the bread will absorb without becoming oily.

---

3 Add the tomatoes, tomato juice, scallions, cucumber, red peppers and chopped basil. Blend.

---

4 Pass through a strainer and dilute with ice cubes. Season.

---

5 Pour the soup into four cold soup bowls, adding a scoop of avocado and basil sherbet and decorating with basil leaves.

For a similar color contrast, try avocado soup with tomato sherbet.

Mousse of Crab
with Pickled Cucumber and a Tomato Coulis

MAIN INGREDIENTS

$\frac{1}{2}$ cucumber, very finely sliced
2 Tbsp chili vinegar
2 Tbsp chopped dill weed
1 Tbsp granulated sugar
white crab meat, cooked, from a 3lb
  crab
4 crab mousses, cold, made with
  the brown crab meat, *page 141*

SAUCE

1c fresh tomato coulis with
  chopped dill added, *page 147*

PRESENTATION

2 tomatoes, peeled, seeded and cut
  into diamond shapes
4 cucumber 'barrels', *page 151*
  chopped chives

---

1 Soak the cucumber in vinegar, dill weed and sugar for at least 20 minutes.

---

2 Sift through the white crab meat and remove any pieces of shell.

---

3 Drain the cucumber.

---

4 Turn the crab mousses onto four chilled plates, and place the white crab meat on top of the mousses.

---

5 Pour tomato coulis around the mousses, and cover the sides of the mousses and the tomato coulis with overlapping slices of cucumber. Decorate.

Drain the cucumber slices well, or pat them with paper towels. Juices running into the sauce tend to dilute it and make it taste somewhat insipid.

Salad of Raw Scallops with Mango, Melon and Snow Peas and a Sesame Oil Dressing

MAIN INGREDIENTS

12 scallop corals, whole
2 Tbsp dry white wine
12 fresh scallops, thinly sliced
1oz pickled ginger, julienned
¼lb snow peas, blanched
1 small Ogen or Charentais melon,
   scooped into balls with a
   parisienne cutter
1 mango, peeled and julienned
2 tomatoes, peeled, seeded and
   julienned
salt and white pepper

DRESSING

¾c sesame oil dressing, *page 146*

PRESENTATION

4 asparagus tips, cooked and
   halved lengthwise

---

1 Blanch the scallop corals for 1 minute in dry white wine, and allow to cool. Marinate the scallops with the pickled ginger for 20 minutes.

---

2 Drain the scallops and ginger to remove all pickling solution. Season.

---

3 Toss all main ingredients in sesame oil dressing.

---

4 Divide between four cold plates. Decorate with the asparagus.

Poach the scallops for a minute or two if eating them raw does not appeal. This should be done after marinating.

HANBURY YOLK
Poached Egg served on an Artichoke with Seafood and a Smoked Cod's Roe Sauce

MAIN INGREDIENTS

4 artichoke hearts, cooked
4 eggs, soft-poached
2 scallops, shelled and halved
   horizontally
4 langostinos, cooked and shelled
1 lobster tail, cooked and cut into 4
   medallions
$4 \times \frac{1}{2}$oz smoked salmon rolls
4 oysters, shelled
8 mussels, cooked and shelled
2oz Sevruga caviar

SAUCE

$1\frac{1}{2}$c cold smoked cod's roe sauce,
   page 146

PRESENTATION

4 cherry tomatoes, peeled
4 broccoli florets, cooked
8 snow peas, blanched
1 tsp salmon's eggs, soaked in cold
   water

1 Divide three-quarters of the sauce between four chilled plates.

2 Place an artichoke heart on each and top this with a cold poached egg.

3 Spoon a little of the remaining sauce over the eggs, and place one each of the different fish on top, leaving the caviar until last.

4 Decorate with tomatoes, broccoli, snow peas and salmon's eggs.

A favorite dish of Marika Hanbury-Tenison to whom it is dedicated.

JOSEPHINE'S DELIGHT
Trio of Mousses with Caviar Smoked Salmon and Scallops

MAIN INGREDIENTS

12 half egg shells, rinsed and dried
(use four of the eggs for the
creamed egg mousse)
6 Tbsp creamed egg mousse, *page
141*
1 oz Beluga caviar
6 Tbsp smoked salmon mousse,
page 147
$\frac{1}{4}$lb smoked salmon, diced
6 Tbsp cold scallop mousse, *page
146*
2 scallops, diced and marinated in
lime juice
1 tsp dropped chives

PRESENTATION

lettuce or other salad leaves
lemon wedges

---

1 Fill four egg shells with creamed egg mousse and top with caviar.

---

2 Fill four egg shells with smoked salmon mousse and top with diced
smoked salmon.

---

3 Fill four egg shells with scallop mousse and top with diced scallop
and chives.

---

4 Decorate with lettuce leaves. Serve with lemon wedges.

---

*Inspired by Michel Guérard. If Josephine's extravagance seems a little too
much, fill the egg shells with any mousse or delight and top with sieved egg
yolk or egg white.*

Oysters and Caviar with poached Quail's Eggs and a Sour Cream Dressing

MAIN INGREDIENTS
12 oysters, shelled: retain deeper
   half of shell
24 quail's eggs, soft-poached in
   acidulated water, *page 155*
2oz Sevruga caviar

SAUCE
¾c sour cream dressing, *page 147*

PRESENTATION
seaweed
1 hard-boiled egg yolk, sieved
1 tsp chopped chives
ice cubes

---

1 In each dish place three oyster shells on a bed of ice cubes and
   seaweed.

---

2 On each shell put two quail's eggs and coat them with a small
   amount of dressing.

---

3 Top with the oysters and caviar. Sprinkle with sieved egg and chives.

The oysters can be poached, or other shellfish used as a substitute.

Patchwork of Salmon and Sea Bass with a Beef Tartare and Cilantro

MAIN INGREDIENTS

5oz beef tenderloin, finely chopped
   but not minced
1 shallot, very finely chopped
1 tsp finely chopped cilantro
1 raw egg yolk
$\frac{1}{2}$ tsp Dijon mustard
$\frac{1}{2}$ tsp granulated sugar
5 Tbsp virgin olive oil
juice of $\frac{1}{2}$ lemon
dash of Worcester sauce
dash of Tabasco sauce
5oz fillet of fresh salmon, skinned
5oz fillet of sea bass, skinned
1 Tbsp olive oil
juice of 1 lime
rock salt and black pepper

PRESENTATION

2 hard-boiled egg yolks, chopped
1 tsp chopped chives
1 Tbsp salmon's eggs
16 cilantro leaves

---

1 Make a tartare by mixing the beef with chopped shallot and cilantro leaves.

---

2 Make a mayonnaise-type dressing by mixing together the egg yolk, mustard and sugar. Gradually add the olive oil drop by drop. Season with lemon juice, Worcester sauce, Tabasco sauce, salt and pepper. Add as much dressing to meat as desired.

---

3 Slice the fish fillets into fine, almost transparent strips. Arrange carefully in a patchwork pattern around four chilled plates. Paint the fish with a fine coating of olive oil and sprinkle with lime juice. Place the beef in the middle of the plates, and surround it with chopped egg yolk. Decorate with chives, salmon's eggs and cilantro. Serve with rock salt and black pepper.

The demand for raw fish becomes greater each week: one of the next restaurant trends may well be towards Westernized Japanese food.

Roulade of Raw Salmon and Turbot with a Spinach Cream and Mint

MAIN INGREDIENTS

2 × ¼lb salmon fillets, skinned and
  flattened
2 Tbsp chopped dill weed
1 Tbsp aquavit, *page 149*
¼c granulated sugar
2 × ¼lb turbot fillets, skinned and
  flattened
juice of 1 lime
½lb fresh spinach leaves, blanched,
  central rib removed
salt and white pepper

SAUCE

1½c cold spinach cream, *page 147*

PRESENTATION

4 tomatoes, peeled, seeded and
  diced
1 Tbsp chopped mint

---

1 Earlier in the day, marinate the salmon in the dill, aquavit, sugar, salt and pepper.

---

2 One and a half hours ahead, marinate the turbot in lime juice, salt and pepper.

---

3 Make two sandwiches of spinach leaves between turbot and salmon. Trim the edges and roll up like jelly rolls. Wrap the rolls tightly in foil to keep them in shape, and refrigerate for 1 hour.

---

4 Cut through the foil rolls producing a total of twelve slices. Remove the foil. Spoon spinach cream onto chilled plates. Arrange three slices of fish roulade on each plate and decorate with the tomato and chopped mint.

Raw fish may seem daunting, but the texture in this dish is similar to that of smoked salmon.

Nest of Smoked Salmon and Leeks with Soft-Boiled Quail's Eggs and a Smoked Cod's Roe Sauce

MAIN INGREDIENTS

2 leeks, julienned and cooked
6oz smoked salmon, cut in fine
  strips
2 Tbsp walnut oil dressing, *page
  148*
16 quail's eggs, soft-boiled

SAUCE

¾c cold smoked cod's roe sauce,
  page 146

PRESENTATION

1 tsp chopped chives

1 On each of four plates, make a nest of leek julienne and smoked salmon strips, spooning a little dressing over the top.

2 Place four eggs on each of the four nests. Top with smoked cod's roe sauce and sprinkle with chives.

Paper-Thin Raw Beef
with Rock Salt and Oysters

MAIN INGREDIENTS

$\frac{3}{4}$lb beef tenderloin, divided into four
    equal pieces and flattened
12 oysters, shelled: reserve
    strained oyster juice
rock salt

SAUCE

$\frac{3}{4}$c dill mayonnaise, *page 142*: peel
    of lemons used in making
    mayonnaise should be kept for
    decoration

PRESENTATION

peel of 2 lemons, julienned and
    blanched
sprigs of dill weed

---

1 Spread the paper-thin pieces of beef on four cold plates. Sprinkle with salt crystals.

---

2 Place three oysters on each piece of beef, and sprinkle with a little strained oyster juice. Decorate the oysters with lemon peel and dill sprigs. Serve the dill mayonnaise separately.

The textures of these raw ingredients are the attraction of the dish.

Whole Poached Pear
with a Leek and Roquefort Mousse
and a Watercress Cream

MAIN INGREDIENTS

4 Comice pears, peeled and
  poached
6 Tbsp leek and Roquefort mousse,
  page 143
1 leek, julienned and cooked

SAUCES

1½c cold watercress cream, *page*
  148
4 Tbsp cold Roquefort cream, *page*
  146

PRESENTATION

1 bunch watercress, washed and
  dried
2 Tbsp walnut oil dressing, *page*
  148

---

1 Core each pear, starting from the base and leaving the stalks
  attached.

---

2 Pipe the hollows full of mousse and put a little mousse in the center
  of each of four chilled plates for the pears to stand on.

---

3 Put one pear in the middle of each plate and surround it with leek
  julienne and watercress cream.

---

4 Trickle Roquefort cream over the pears.

---

5 Dip the watercress leaves into the walnut oil dressing and arrange
  them around the edge of each plate.

Chilled Leek with Wild Mushrooms and a Dill Cream

MAIN INGREDIENTS

4 young leeks, cooked, refreshed,
drained and seasoned
$\frac{1}{2}$c wild mushroom duxelle, *page
142*

SAUCE

$\frac{3}{4}$c cold dill cream, *page 142*

PRESENTATION

sprigs of dill weed

Arrange as shown in the photograph.

Increases the interest of a leek quite remarkably.

MOUSSE of JERUSALEM ARTICHOKES with a Salad of Mussels and Vegetables

MAIN INGREDIENTS
1 lb mussels
$\frac{3}{4}$ c dry white wine
2 shallots, chopped
2 cloves garlic, chopped
1 bay leaf
1 lb Jerusalem artichokes
3 sheets gelatin
$\frac{3}{4}$ c whipping cream
3 egg whites
2 artichoke hearts, cooked and
  diced
2 tomatoes, peeled, seeded and
  diced
4 scallions, cut into 1 inch lengths
salt and white pepper

DRESSING
$\frac{3}{4}$ c walnut oil dressing, *page 148*

PRESENTATION
fresh herbs

---

1 Wash the mussels thoroughly and add the wine, shallots, garlic and bay leaf, cover and cook until open. Shell and allow to cool. Discard any that have not opened. Reserve the cooking liquid.

---

2 Peel and slice the Jerusalem artichokes and simmer for 15 minutes in plenty of mussel stock and water.

---

3 Soften the gelatin in a third of the cream. Drain the artichokes and purée them while still warm with the gelatin mixture. Season, turn out into a bowl and allow to cool.

---

4 Whip the remaining cream to soft peaks. In a separate bowl whip the egg whites to a similar consistency. Fold the whipped cream and then the whipped egg whites into the Jerusalem artichoke purée.

---

5 Add the mussels to the purée and put the mixture into one large mold or several smaller ones. Refrigerate for 2 hours.

---

6 Toss the artichoke hearts, tomatoes and scallions lightly in the dressing.

---

7 Dip the molds in hot water for 3 seconds, and turn the mousses out onto cold plates. Surround the mousses with the vegetables and decorate.

Salad of Smoked Chicken and Lobster with a Walnut Oil Dressing

MAIN INGREDIENTS

$\frac{1}{2}$ cucumber, peeled, seeded and cut into sticks
julienned cucumber peel
4 scallions, cut to the same length as cucumber sticks
1 head Belgian endive, julienned just before use
3 tomatoes, peeled, seeded and julienned
julienne of blanched lemon rind: use lemon juice for the dressing
1 smoked chicken breast, skinned, boned and julienned
1lb lobster tail, cooked, shelled and diced
salt and white pepper

DRESSING

$\frac{3}{4}$c walnut oil dressing, *page 148*

PRESENTATION

1 pear, peeled and poached
2 tomatoes, peeled, seeded and diced
lamb's lettuce leaves, dipped into dressing

---

1 Sprinkle salt over the cucumber sticks. After 30 minutes, drain and rinse the cucumber to remove excess salt. Dry on paper towels.

---

2 Toss the main ingredients in walnut oil dressing. Season. Divide between four small bowls.

---

3 Quarter and core the cooked pear. Slice and arrange around the plate with the lamb's lettuce (dipped in dressing) and the diced tomato.

Julienne of smoked ham would be just as delicious if the chicken were unavailable. Try experimenting with different dressings.

Warm Cocktail of Garden Vegetables with a Cold Mousse of Eggplant

MAIN INGREDIENTS
6 medium-sized eggplants
1 shallot, chopped
1 clove garlic, chopped
9 sheets gelatin
2c double cream
1½c cold jellied stock, *page 148*
4 egg whites
salt and paprika

DRESSING
¾c walnut oil dressing, *page 148*

PRESENTATION
vegetables, trimmed or sliced and
 blanched: choose from
 cauliflower, broccoli, asparagus,
 tomatoes, snow peas, young
 green beans, carrots, cucumber,
 zucchini, artichokes

---

1 Peel the eggplants and keep the skin. Roughly dice the flesh, and
   cook it in very little water with the shallot and garlic for about 20
   minutes or until soft enough to go into the food processor or
   blender. Purée until smooth.

---

2 Meanwhile, soften seven sheets of gelatin in a third of the cream
   and add them to the warm purée. Strain through a fine sieve.
   Season and allow to cool. Soften the remaining gelatin in cold
   water.

---

3 Simmer the eggplant peel in the jellied stock with the two sheets of
   gelatin for about 8 to 10 minutes. Reserve the stock, keeping it at
   room temperature so it cools but does not set. Line four molds with
   the eggplant peel and chill.

---

4 Whip the remaining cream to soft peaks. In a separate bowl whip
   the egg whites to a similar consistency. Fold first the whipped cream
   and then the whipped egg whites into the purée. Spoon the mixture
   into molds and allow to set in the refrigerator for 2 hours.

---

5 After 2 hours dip the molds in hot water for 10 seconds and turn
   them out onto a rack. Coat the cold mousses with the jellied stock.

---

6 Warm the vegetables in the dressing, tossing them gently to ensure
   that they are glazed all over. Season. Place a mousse in the center of
   each of four plates and arrange the vegetables round them. Serve
   immediately.

Warm Salad of Green Leaves with Avocado, Quail's Eggs and Roquefort

MAIN INGREDIENTS

6 Tbsp walnut oil
4 Tbsp lardoons
3 Tbsp croûtons
1 avocado, peeled and sliced
1 artichoke heart, cooked and
 julienned
12 quail's eggs, soft-boiled and
 shelled
6oz Roquefort, crumbled
salad leaves, washed and dried:
 choose from lamb's lettuce, curly
 endive and dandelion
1 head Belgian endive, wiped
salt and black pepper

SAUCES

¾c cold Roquefort cream, *page 146*
4 Tbsp walnut oil dressing, *page
 148*

PRESENTATION

fresh herbs: choose from chervil,
 chives, nasturtium and basil
1 tomato, peeled, seeded and
 julienned

---

1 Heat the walnut oil. Fry the lardoons until crisp, then add the
 croûtons and cook until golden brown. Drain off three-quarters of
 the oil. Add the avocado and artichoke heart. Toss once or twice to
 combine the ingredients. Add eggs and Roquefort, season, and heat
 until the cheese begins to melt. Drain with a slotted spoon.

---

2 Deglaze the pan with the walnut oil dressing. Toss the salad leaves
 in the warm dressing and arrange between four warm plates.
 Sprinkle the other ingredients on top. Spoon the Roquefort cream
 over the salad, and decorate with herbs and tomato. Serve
 immediately.

---

*These crisp salads with warm dressings are really special, but do not cut
corners: make them just before serving.*

YOUNG ZUCCHINI AND THEIR FLOWERS
stuffed with a Wild Mushroom Mousse

MAIN INGREDIENTS
8 small zucchini with flowers
  attached
$\frac{1}{2}$c wild mushroom mousse, *page*
  149

SAUCE
$1\frac{1}{2}$c warm wild mushroom sauce,
page 149

PRESENTATION
$\frac{1}{2}$ stick ($\frac{1}{4}$c) unsalted butter, clarified
1 shallot, finely chopped
16 small morels, washed and dried
2 Tbsp cognac
4 cherry tomatoes, peeled
salt and black pepper

---

1 Rinse the inside of the zucchini flowers to remove insects. Do not soak. Fit a piping bag with a large straight nozzle and fill with mushroom mousse.

---

2 Carefully pipe the zucchini flowers four-fifths full of mousse and then fold the ends of the petals to enclose the mousse.

---

3 Steam the zucchini for approximately 10 minutes, just enough to cook the mousse without overcooking the zucchini.

---

4 Heat the butter, add the shallot and cook over gentle heat until softened. Add morels and continue to cook over low heat for 5 minutes. Season.

---

5 Turn up the heat. Pour in the cognac, ignite and burn off all alcohol. When the flames have died down, remove the morels and keep warm. Strain the pan juices into the sauce.

---

6 Spoon the sauce onto warm plates. Slice the zucchini lengthwise to within $\frac{1}{2}$ inch of the flower and fan out on the plates. Decorate with the morels and tomatoes.

Treat the flowers carefully: they are delicate and very susceptible to tearing or falling off.

Twice-Cooked Duck Foie Gras with Raspberry Vinegar

MAIN INGREDIENTS

8 slices fresh duck foie gras
4 Savoy cabbage leaves, blanched,
   central rib removed
salt and white pepper

SAUCE

2 Tbsp raspberry vinegar
2 Tbsp port
5 Tbsp golden veal stock, *page 148*
$\frac{1}{2}$ stick ($\frac{1}{4}$c) cold unsalted butter,
   diced

PRESENTATION

1 box fresh raspberries

---

1 Heat a large frying pan and add the slices of foie gras. Seal them for
   15 seconds on each side. Season.

---

2 Remove four slices and wrap them individually in cabbage leaves.
   Steam the parcels for 2 minutes. The four slices remaining in the
   frying pan should be cooked for a further 20 seconds on each side.
   Remove them and keep warm on paper towels.

---

3 Add the vinegar and port to the frying pan to loosen sediment on
   base. Stir to combine. Add the veal stock. Bring to a boil. Season.
   Stir in the cold butter a piece at a time until emulsified.

---

4 Place the unwrapped foie gras slices in the centers of four warm
   plates and coat with the sauce. Top with the cabbage leaf parcels
   and decorate with raspeberries.

---

*The unique flavor of fresh duck foie gras makes any substitute a
disappointing second. However, a similar contrast between ingredients can
be achieved by using calf's liver or chicken livers as alternatives to the foie
gras.*

Warm Salad of French Leaves with Langostinos and Sweetbreads

MAIN INGREDIENTS

4 Tbsp lardoons
5 Tbsp walnut oil
3 Tbsp croûtons
¾ stick (6 Tbsp) unsalted butter,
  clarified
½ lb calf's sweetbreads, cooked
16 langostino tails, cooked and
  shelled
fresh herbs, roughly chopped:
  choose from nasturtium, parsley,
  chives, chervil, basil
lemon juice
salad leaves washed and dried:
  choose from lamb's lettuce, curly
  endive, radicchio and dandelion
salt and white pepper

DRESSING

¾c walnut oil dressing, *page 148*

PRESENTATION

12 cherry tomatoes, peeled
1 orange, peeled and segmented

---

1 Fry the lardoons in hot walnut oil for 2 minutes, stirring well. When they begin to crisp, add croûtons and fry until golden brown. Drain and set aside.

---

2 At the same time heat the butter in another pan and sauté the sweetbreads for 2 to 3 minutes, turning once. Add the langostino tails and a third of the herbs. Toss together, season with pepper and lemon juice, remove and drain. Deglaze the pan with the walnut oil dressing.

---

3 Put the salad leaves in a bowl, sprinkle with another third of the herbs and some salt and pepper. Mix with a little warm walnut oil dressing, enough to coat but not drown them.

---

4 Divide the salad between four warm plates. Scatter with lardoons and croûtons. Arrange the langostino tails and sweetbreads on top, and sprinkle with the remaining herbs. Decorate and serve immediately.

A Warm Woodland Salad with Pigeon and Wild Mushrooms

MAIN INGREDIENTS

5 Tbsp walnut oil
1 Tbsp lardoons
3 Tbsp croûtons
4 pigeon breasts
¾ stick (6 Tbsp) unsalted butter, clarified
1 shallot, chopped
1 clove garlic, chopped
4 oyster mushrooms
salad leaves, washed and dried: choose from lamb's lettuce, curly endive and radicchio
salt and white pepper

DRESSING

3 Tbsp walnut oil dressing, *page 148*

PRESENTATION

1 orange, peeled and segmented
8 lychees, peeled and pitted

---

1 Heat the walnut oil and fry the lardoons in it until starting to crisp. Add the croûtons and fry them until golden brown.

---

2 Season the pigeon breasts. Brown them in 2 tablespoons of the butter. Roast in a hot oven for 6 minutes.

---

3 Sweat the shallots and garlic in the remaining butter until soft but not brown. Add the oyster mushrooms, raise the heat and sauté quickly for 1 minute on each side. Season. Drain and keep warm. Add the walnut oil dressing to pan and warm.

---

4 Carve the pigeon breasts into thin strips. Toss the salad leaves in warm walnut oil dresing and divide between four warm plates. Sprinkle lardoons and croûtons over the salad and top with pigeon strips and oyster mushrooms. Decorate with orange segments and lychees. Serve immediately.

Other game birds can be used as substitutes for pigeon.

Filo Pastry 'Frying Pan'
with Wild Mushrooms and Garden Vegetables

MAIN INGREDIENTS

$1\frac{1}{2}$ sticks ($\frac{3}{4}$c) unsalted butter,
 clarified
8 sheets filo pastry, and another 2
 sheets cut in half horizontally
1 shallot, finely chopped
vegetables, trimmed to similar sizes
 and blanched: choose from
 young carrots with 1 inch of
 foliage, asparagus tips, snow
 peas, young green beans,
 broccoli, zucchini, young leeks,
 cauliflower

wild mushrooms, washed, dried
 and sliced:
 $\frac{1}{2}$c chanterelles
 $\frac{1}{2}$c oyster mushrooms
 $\frac{1}{2}$c wood hedgehog mushrooms
 $\frac{1}{2}$c horns of plenty
salt and black pepper

SAUCE

$1\frac{1}{2}$c warm wild mushroom sauce,
 page 149

PRESENTATION

4 cherry tomatoes, peeled
1oz truffle, julienned

1 To make filo pastry 'frying pans', brush one whole pastry sheet with
   melted butter and fold in two, see the diagram, *page 138*. Lay it in a
   small iron frying pan, mold to the shape of the pan, and trim off the
   excess. Butter a half sheet, roll it up to make a 'handle' and lay it
   partly in the pan but with 3 inches extending up the real pan
   handle.

2 To secure the 'handle', cover the 'pan' area with another sheet,
   folded. Trim this to shape and prick all over with a fork. Brush once
   more with butter. Bake, without removing from the real pan, in a
   hot oven for about 12 minutes, or until crisp and brown.

3 Detach the cooked 'pan' gently from the real pan, and make three
   more 'pans' in the same way.

4 Meanwhile, 5 minutes before the last 'pan' is finished, start cooking
   the vegetables. Add the shallot to the remaining butter and cook in
   a large frying pan over gentle heat until softened. Increase the heat
   and add all the mushrooms. Cook for $1\frac{1}{2}$ minutes and then add the
   other vegetables. Stir-fry until heated through. Season.

5 Reheat the pastry 'frying pans' in a warm oven for 3 minutes. Place
   them gently on warm plates. When the vegetables are ready, check
   the seasoning and arrange them in the 'pans'. Top with truffle
   julienne and tomatoes. Serve the sauce separately.

Warm Salad of Belgian Endive with Scallops, Tomato and Red Mullet

MAIN INGREDIENTS

4 medium-sized tomatoes, peeled
4c lamb's lettuce leaves, washed
  and dried
2 heads Belgian endive
$\frac{1}{2}$ lemon
8 small red mullet fillets, cut into
  long strips
4 scallops, each shelled and sliced
  into three horizontally
$\frac{1}{2}$ stick (4 Tbsp) unsalted butter,
  clarified
1 Tbsp olive oil
salt and white pepper

SAUCES

$\frac{3}{4}$c cold dill cream mixed with 2
  Tbsp of cold spinach cream,
  pages 142 and 147
2 Tbsp hazelnut oil dressing,
  page 143

PRESENTATION

sprigs of dill weed

---

1 Cut the tops off the tomatoes. Scoop out the seeds with a parisienne cutter and lightly salt the insides. Turn the tomatoes upside down and leave for 30 minutes.

---

2 Pull the Belgian endive leaves apart by hand. (Try not to cut Belgian endive with a knife unless it is to be used immediately: otherwise it discolors.)

---

3 Rinse the insides of the tomatoes with cold water, drain and fill with the dill and spinach creams.

---

4 Squeeze the lemon over the red mullet fillets and scallops. Season. Sauté the red mullet fillets in butter and oil for 2 minutes, skin side down, then turn them over. Add the scallops, cooking for 20 seconds each side. Remove and keep warm. Deglaze the pan with the hazelnut oil dressing.

---

5 Toss the salad leaves in the warm dressing and arrange on four warm plates around the tomatoes. Arrange the mullet and scallops and decorate with dill. Serve immediately.

Oysters
served warm with Spinach and Dill

MAIN INGREDIENTS

16 oysters, shelled: reserve strained
   oyster juice
1 Tbsp dry white vermouth
$\frac{1}{2}$ shallot, chopped
16 spinach leaves, blanched,
   drained and central rib removed
$\frac{1}{2}$c spinach mousse, *page 147*
$\frac{1}{8}$ stick (2 Tbsp) unsalted butter,
   clarified
salt and white pepper

SAUCE

$1\frac{1}{2}$c warm dill sauce, *page 142*

PRESENTATION

2 tsp salmon's eggs
8 sprigs of dill weed

---

1 Heat the oyster juices and vermouth with the shallot. Poach the oysters in the liquid for 30 seconds. Allow to cool in the liquid. Use the strained liquid as part of the stock required in the dill sauce.

---

2 Spread out eight spinach leaves. Put a teaspoon of spinach mousse in the center of each leaf, and a cooked oyster on top of the mousse. Season. Smooth the mousse around the oyster. Enclose with the spinach leaf, squeezing the parcels gently to mold into neat shapes. Steam the parcels for 6 minutes. Steam remaining oysters for 2 minutes.

---

3 Warm the butter and in it heat the remaining spinach leaves. Season.

---

4 Arrange two spinach leaves on each of four warmed plates. Top with the unwrapped oysters and a spoonful of dill sauce. Add two oyster parcels to each plate. Garnish with salmon's eggs and fresh dill. Serve the remaining sauce separately.

Dill is the perfect herb for shellfish.

WHOLE MORELS WITH TRUFFLES
and a Morel Sauce

MAIN INGREDIENTS

12 large and 12 small morels,
   washed thoroughly; use stalks
   for mousse
$\frac{1}{4}$c morel mousse, *page 145*
$\frac{1}{4}$ stick (2 Tbsp) unsalted butter,
   clarified
12 truffle slices (optional)
salt and white pepper

SAUCE

1$\frac{1}{2}$c warm morel sauce, *page 145*
3oz fresh foie gras, diced

1 Fill the 12 larger morels with the mousse, using a small piping bag. Season and steam for approximately 8 minutes. Keep warm.

2 Sauté the smaller morels in butter for approximately 3 minutes, tossing regularly. Season. Add the truffle slices and the larger morels for the last 30 seconds.

3 For the sauce, instead of finishing with butter, fold in the finely diced foie gras – it will quickly reduce. Stir from time to time to emulsify the foie gras juices with the wild mushroom sauce. Strain.

4 Divide the mushroom sauce between four warm plates. Arrange the morels and truffle.

Warm Salad of Lobster and Foie Gras with Red and Green Salads

MAIN INGREDIENTS

1 lb live lobster
$\frac{1}{2}$ lb fresh duck foie gras, cut into 8
   slices
salad leaves washed and dried:
   radicchio and lamb's lettuce
salt and black pepper

DRESSING

3 Tbsp raspberry vinegar
1 shallot, finely chopped
$\frac{1}{4}$ stick (2 Tbsp) cold unsalted
   butter, diced

PRESENTATION

1 orange, peeled and segmented
1 box raspberries
2 Tbsp fresh chopped herbs: choose
   from chives, mint, basil, chervil

---

1 Twenty minutes in advance, cook the lobster in a boiling court-bouillon for 10 minutes, Keep it warm in the liquid.

---

2 Season the foie gras slices and fry them in a hot pan for 20 seconds on each side; no extra fat is needed. Put them on paper towels and keep warm. Reserve the fat in the pan.

---

3 Shell the lobster and divide the meat from claws and body into four portions.

---

4 Sweat the shallot in the fat from the foie gras over a low heat. Raise the heat and add the raspberry vinegar, then the butter. Stir until emulsified. Toss the salad leaves in this warm dressing. Arrange them on four warm plates.

---

5 Top with lobster and slices of foie gras, and decorate with orange segments, raspeberries and herbs.

Trio of Sea Urchins with Hen's, Gull's and Quail's Eggs

MAIN INGREDIENTS

12 sea urchins
1 shallot
$\frac{1}{2}$ clove garlic
$\frac{1}{4}$ stick (2 Tbsp) unsalted butter, clarified
4 gull's eggs
7 Tbsp heavy cream
4 medium-sized hen's eggs
1 tsp grated horseradish
acidulated water, *page 155*

8 quail's eggs
1 lb rock salt
salt and black pepper

PRESENTATION

urchin's roe
2 tsp chopped chives
2 oz smoked salmon
1 oz Beluga caviar

---

1 Cut open the urchins with special cutters or kitchen scissors. Cut off the top with the 'eye', leaving a perfect rounded container. Strain off the juices and the orange roe and reserve both.

---

2 Clean the urchin shells thoroughly, making quite sure there are no loose spines left inside. Spread the rock salt on four plates and put them with the shells to warm in the oven.

---

3 Sweat the chopped shallot and garlic in butter until soft but not brown. Add three-quarters of the roe and toss gently for 1 minute. Divide this mixture between the twelve shells and return them to the oven. Reserve remaining roe for presentation.

---

4 Break a gull's egg carefully onto the roe in four of the shells. Season, and top each with a tablespoon of cream mixed with urchin juice. Bake in a medium oven in a bain-marie for about 6 to 8 minutes. Decorate with the reserved urchin roe.

---

5 Scramble hen's eggs (use method for scrambled quail's eggs on *page 67*). Divide between another four of the roe-filled urchin shells and top with salmon and chives.

---

6 Poach quail's eggs (use method on *page 67*). Place two poached eggs in each of the remaining roe-filled urchin shells and top with a tablespoon of cream mixed with urchin juice. Decorate with caviar.

---

7 Keep the filled urchin eggs warm on the plates of hot rock salt. Serve one of each sort on each of the four plates.

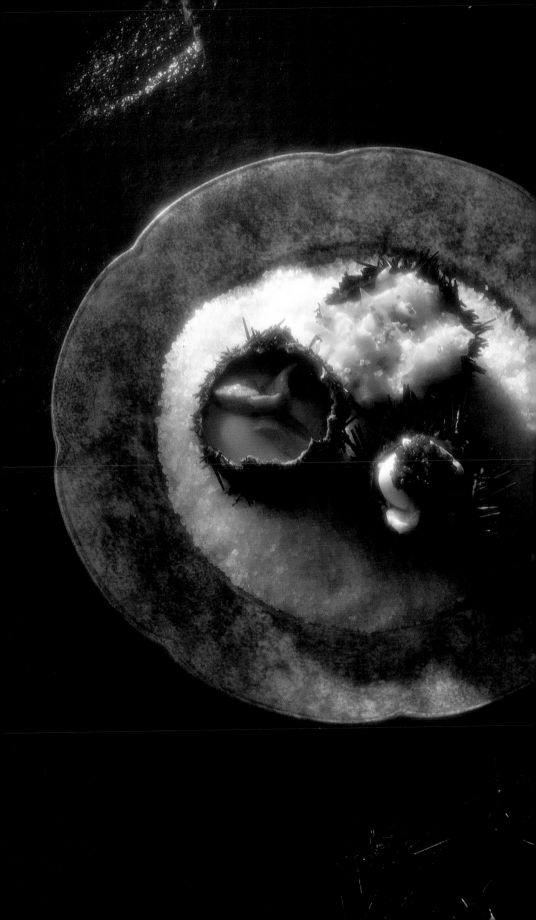

Duck Magret with Oysters
and a Champagne Sauce

MAIN INGREDIENTS

16 oysters, shelled; reserve strained
    oyster juices
8 spinach leaves, blanched and
    central rib removed
6 Tbsp spinach mousse, *page 147*
$\frac{1}{2}$lb duck magret, fatty skin removed
    and diced
salt and black pepper

SAUCES

$\frac{3}{4}$c warm champagne sauce, *page*
    140
6 Tbsp walnut oil dressing, *page*
    148

PRESENTATION

sprigs of dill weed
2 tomatoes, peeled, seeded and
    quartered

---

1 Blanch eight of the oysters for 1 minute in their juices. Allow to cool.

---

2 Spread the spinach leaves over a flat surface and place a teaspoon of spinach mousse in the center of each. Top with a blanched oyster and a second teaspoon of mousse. Fold the leaf to enclose the parcel. Steam the parcels for approximately 8 minutes.

---

3 At the same time, put the duck magret in a roasting tin, scatter the diced skin over it, season and roast for 8 to 12 minutes. Remove it from the oven and keep the duck warm. Drain the melted fats from the roasting pan and return the pan to the oven with the skin in it. When crisp, remove the skin, drain again and deglaze the pan with the walnut oil dressing.

---

4 Heat the champagne sauce and add the remaining eight oysters. Warm through but do not allow to boil. Cut the duck into julienne strips and toss them in the warm walnut oil dressing.

---

5 Place the duck julienne and crisp skin in center of warm plates. Arrange the other ingredients and decorate.

Long Island duckling can be used as a substitute for duck magret.

Warm Salad of Dandelion
with Lamb's Kidneys and Chicken Livers

MAIN INGREDIENTS

$\frac{1}{2}$lb chicken livers
4 lamb's kidneys in suet
4 Tbsp walnut oil
4 Tbsp lardoons
3 Tbsp croûtons
$\frac{1}{4}$ stick (2 Tbsp) unsalted butter,
  clarified
2 sage leaves
4c dandelion leaves, washed and
  dried
salt and black pepper

DRESSING

$\frac{3}{4}$c walnut oil dressing, *page 148*

PRESENTATION

1 bunch watercress, washed and
  drained
4 tomatoes, peeled, seeded and
  quartered
2 oranges, peeled and segmented

---

1 One hour before serving, soak the chicken livers in iced water.

---

2 Twenty minutes before serving, drain and dry the livers. Trim the suet from the kidney leaving a thin covering. Season.

---

3 Cook the kidneys in a hot oven for about 8 to 12 minutes, more if preferred well done. Remove from the oven but keep warm.

---

4 Heat the oil and add the lardoons. Cook until starting to crisp, turning regularly. Add the croûtons and cook until golden brown. Drain and keep warm.

---

5 Strain the oil and return it to the pan. Add the butter and heat. Sauté the chicken livers with the sage leaves, turning regularly. Cook for 3 to 5 minutes, season and drain. Remove three-quarters of the juices and add the dressing to the remainder in the pan.

---

6 Toss the dandelion leaves in the warm dressing, and divide onto four warm plates. Sprinkle with lardoons and croûtons. Slice the kidneys and arrange on top of the salad with the livers.

---

7 Decorate with watercress, tomato and orange.

Curly endive would be a good substitute for dandelion.

Quail's Eggs
with Caviar, Smoked Salmon and Truffle

MAIN PRESENTATION
12 round croûtons, 1 inch diameter
6 cherry tomatoes, peeled and
  halved

1 tsp chopped chives
12 spinach leaves, blanched,
  central rib removed
3 Tbsp leek, julienned and cooked

---

1 SCRAMBLED QUAIL'S EGGS

8 quail's eggs
1 Tbsp heavy cream
$\frac{1}{8}$ stick (1 Tbsp) unsalted
  butter, clarified
1 tsp grated horseradish
salt and white pepper

PRESENTATION
2oz smoked salmon

Heat the butter, cream and horseradish. Crack the eggs into a cup
and break up with a fork. Add the eggs to saucepan and cook to the
right consistency. Season. Keep warm.

---

2 POACHED QUAIL'S EGGS

4 quail's eggs
acidulated water, *page 155*

PRESENTATION
2 Tbsp horseradish cream, *page 143*
1oz Beluga caviar

Crack each egg onto a spoon and slide gently into simmering
acidulated water. Cook $1\frac{1}{2}$ minutes. Drain, trim and keep warm.
When serving, top with horseradish cream.

---

3 FRIED QUAIL'S EGGS

4 quail's eggs
$\frac{1}{4}$ stick (2 Tbsp) unsalted
  butter, clarified

PRESENTATION
4 slices truffle, julienned

Fry the eggs gently in butter. Season. Drain and keep warm.

---

4 Gently fry the croûtons in the same butter as the fried eggs.

---

5 Arrange the eggs on the croûtons. Decorate each with smoked
  salmon, caviar or truffle, and sprinkle the scrambled and poached
  eggs with chopped chives.

---

6 Arrange on four warm plates together with the tomato halves,
  spinach, leek julienne and any remaining smoked salmon.

MÉNAGE À TROIS
Three hot cheese pastry parcels

MAIN INGREDIENTS

(Makes 24 parcels)

12 sheets filo pastry, each cut in
 half, *page 138*
1 stick ($\frac{1}{2}$c) unsalted butter, clarified

CAMEMBERT AND
CRANBERRY FILLING

Ingredients for each parcel:
1 small piece of Camembert
1 tsp cranberry sauce, *page 151*
pinch of paprika

Place on pastry in above order.

BOURSIN AND SPINACH
FILLING

Ingredients for each parcel:
1 Tbsp spinach mousse, *page 147*
1 tsp Boursin

*Fold Boursin into mousse and place on
pastry.*

LEEK AND ROQUEFORT
FILLING

Ingredients for each parcel:
1 Tbsp leek and Roquefort mousse,
 page 143, omitting gelatin
1 small cube Roquefort cheese

*Place mousse on pastry and the cheese
on top.*

For assembly into filo pastry parcels, see the diagrams on *page 138*.
Just before serving, plunge them into hot deep fat and fry until crisp
and golden, about 3 minutes. Serve with sauce and decorations of
your own choice. More filling suggestions are on *pages 144–5*.

Cream Soup of Wild Mushrooms with Ravioli of Truffle and foie Gras

MAIN INGREDIENTS

2 shallots, finely chopped
1 clove garlic, chopped
1 small potato, peeled and diced
$\frac{1}{4}$ stick (2 Tbsp) unsalted butter, clarified
wild mushrooms: 1c ceps
   1c wood hedgehog mushrooms
   1c chanterelles
   1c oyster mushrooms
1 Tbsp peanut oil
1 bay leaf
2c vegetable stock, *page 148*
$1\frac{1}{2}$c heavy cream
3 Tbsp truffle juice
pinch of grated nutmeg
salt and black pepper

PRESENTATION

12 ravioli filled with truffle and foie gras, *page 146*
4 morels, quartered and sautéed in butter

---

1 Cook the shallot, garlic and potato in the butter over a low heat.

---

2 Sweat the mushrooms in the oil in a large pan until they have released all juices. Add shallot, garlic, potato, bay leaf and vegetable stock. Bring to a boil and simmer for 10 minutes.

---

3 Add the cream and boil for a further 5 minutes. Remove bay leaf. Blend, strain and return to the heat. Skim.

---

4 Add the truffle juice and season with salt, pepper, nutmeg and champagne vinegar. Bring the soup to the boil once more and add the ravioli. Cook for 2 minutes.

---

5 Divide between four warm bowls and decorate with morels.

Field mushrooms can be used as a substitute in this excellent soup.

MINESTRONE OF SHELLFISH AND VEGETABLES
perfumed with fresh Basil

MAIN INGREDIENTS

½ bottle dry white wine
1 shallot, finely chopped
2 cloves garlic, crushed
2 Tbsp finely chopped fresh ginger
1 lb mussels
4 langostinos, live
3c vegetable stock, *page 148*
1 carrot, diced
1 scallion sliced

1 leek, sliced
a few broccoli florets
a few cauliflower florets
1 artichoke heart, cooked and diced
1 tomato, peeled, seeded and diced
8 scallops, shelled and sliced in
   halves horizontally
1 small bunch basil, julienned
1 Tbsp basil butter (optional), *page
   149*
salt and black pepper

1 Boil the wine, shallot, garlic and ginger for 3 minutes. Add the mussels, cover the pan and cook over a high heat until the mussels have opened. Strain through a fine sieve and reserve the juice. Shell the mussels, discarding any that have not opened.

2 Boil the langostinos in vegetable stock for 2 minutes. Strain the liquid into the mussel stock. Shell the langostinos and cut into small slices.

3 Boil the mussel liquid and vegetable stock together. Add the carrot and scallion. Cook for 5 minutes. Add the leek, broccoli and cauliflower. Cook for another 5 minutes.

4 Add the mussels, artichoke, tomato and langostinos. Season. Bring back to a boil, and add the scallops and julienned basil. Serve at once. A little basil butter can be added before serving.

Cream Soup of Mussels and Saffron accompanied by a Julienne of Vegetables

MAIN INGREDIENTS

$\frac{3}{4}$ stick (6 Tbsp) unsalted butter,
   clarified
2 shallots, finely chopped
2 cloves garlic, finely chopped
2 tsp finely chopped fresh ginger
$2\frac{1}{2}$c dry white wine
1 Tbsp soy sauce
$2\frac{1}{2}$pt mussels, cleaned
1 stick celerry, diced
$\frac{1}{2}$ small head fennel, diced
white of 1 leek, diced
1 small potato, diced
1 small carrot, diced
$2\frac{1}{2}$c fish stock, *page 142*
1 bay leaf

sprig of thyme
pinch of saffron stamens, soaked in
   1 Tbsp warm water
$1\frac{1}{2}$c heavy cream
salt, white pepper and grated
   nutmeg

PRESENTATION

1 leek, julienned and blanched
1 carrot, julienned and blanched
1 tomato, peeled, seeded and very
   finely julienned
$\frac{1}{4}$ stick (2 Tbsp) unsalted butter

---

1 Heat the butter in a large saucepan. Add the shallot, garlic and ginger and cook over a low heat until soft but not brown.

---

2 Remove half the mixture to a second saucepan. Add the wine and soy sauce to the first pan and bring to a boil. Add the mussels and cook, covered, for approximately 5 minutes, shaking the pan at regular intervals. When the mussels have opened, shell them, discarding any that remain firmly closed, and strain their stock into the saucepan.

---

3 Add the vegetables from the main ingredients list, the fish stock, bay leaf and thyme to the mussel stock and sweated shallot mixture. Bring to a boil and simmer for approximately 25 minutes or until the vegetables are soft.

---

4 Remove the bay leaf and thyme. Blend the soup and pass through a fine strainer. Return to the heat. Add the saffron stamens. The soup will turn pale yellow. Add the cream, and season with nutmeg, salt and pepper. Do not allow it to boil.

---

5 Gently heat the mussels and presentation ingredients in a little butter. Serve with the soup in warm bowls.

Cream Soup of Chicken and Watercress with floating Watercress 'Islands'

MAIN INGREDIENTS

3c strong chicken stock, *page 141*
1 chicken breast, boned and finely
   diced
2 bunches watercress, washed,
   leaves only: use stalks in
   preparation of stock
1½c heavy cream
2 egg yolks mixed with 2 Tbsp of
   the cream
salt and white pepper

PRESENTATION

handful of watercress leaves,
   blanched
8 egg whites, with pinch of salt
   added

1 Bring the stock to boil and add the chicken. Simmer for 5 minutes.

2 Add two bunches of watercress leaves and the cream. Cook for a further 1 minute and then blend until smooth. Season.

3 Whisk the egg whites to stiff peaks and carefully fold in the handful of blanched watercress leaves. Poach spoonfuls of egg white in lightly salted water, turning once. Remove and drain on paper towels.

4 Reheat the soup. Add the egg yolk and cream mixture. Do not allow it to boil.

5 Serve in warm bowls with floating watercress islands.

FEUILLETÉ OF LANGOSTINO AND ASPARAGUS
with a Minted Orange Sauce

MAIN INGREDIENTS

20 langostino tails, cooked and
  shelled
8 asparagus spears of the same
  length, cooked
4 puff pastry rectangles
  approximately $2\frac{1}{2}$ inches × 1
  inch, cooked
$\frac{1}{4}$ stick (2 Tbsp) unsalted butter,
  clarified
salt and white pepper

SAUCE

$1\frac{1}{2}$c warm minted orange sauce,
  page 145

PRESENTATION

1 tomato, peeled and quartered
1 orange, peeled and segmented
4 sprigs of young mint leaves

1 Heat the langostino tails and asparagus by tossing gently in hot
  butter, or by steaming, or by poaching in a little fish stock. Season.

2 Reheat the pastry rectangles in a hot oven for 1 minute. Split them
  horizontally.

3 Divide the sauce equally between four warmed plates. Put the
  bottom half of the pastry case on the sauce and arrange the
  langostino on top. Replace the pastry lid. Lay the asparagus spears
  in a cross beside the feuilleté and brush with clarified butter.
  Decorate.

For the langostino, you can substitute king prawns.

Fillets of Red Mullet and Turbot with Asparagus and Two Sauces

MAIN INGREDIENTS

8 × 1½oz fillets of turbot, skinned
8 × 1½oz fillets of red mullet, scales
  removed
8 asparagus tips, blanched
juice of ½ lemon
salt and white pepper

SAUCES

¾c warm tomato and basil sauce,
  page 147
¾c warm spinach sauce, *page 147*

PRESENTATION

1 small leek, julienned and
  blanched
1 tomato, skinned, seeded and
  diced
¼ stick (2 Tbsp) unsalted butter,
  clarified

---

1 As far as possible the fish fillets should be trimmed to equal lengths.
Steam fish fillets and asparagus until cooked, 5 to 7 minutes. (Put
the turbot in the steamer just ahead of the mullet, as its flesh is
slightly more dense.) Season with salt, pepper and lemon juice.

---

2 Toss the leek julienned in hot butter. Drain and season.

---

3 Spoon the warm sauces onto warm plates, and arrange the
ingredients as in the photograph.

---

*The small green circles on the plate are thin slices of asparagus – they add
color to the dish.*

MOSAIC OF SALMON AND SOLE
with a Nettle and Sorrel Sauce

MAIN INGREDIENTS

1½lb Dover sole, skinned and filleted
  into four pieces
16 spinach leaves, blanched,
  central rib removed
¾lb salmon fillet, skinned
4 squares aluminium foil, buttered
juice of ½ lemon
salt and white pepper

SAUCE

1½c warm nettle and sorrel sauce,
  page 145

PRESENTATION

2 tsp salmon's eggs, soaked in cold
  water
1 Tbsp chopped chives

---

1 Cut each of the four sole fillets into four equal strips, season with
   salt, pepper and lemon juice, and wrap each strip in a blanched
   spinach leaf. Trim the edges of all sixteen parcels so that they are
   uniform in shape and size.

---

2 Cut the salmon fillet into sixteen strips as nearly as possible the
   same size as the sole. Season with salt, pepper and lemon juice.

---

3 Weave four strips of each sort of fish into a square on each of the
   sheets of buttered foil.

---

4 Steam the fish on the foil for 6 to 8 minutes.

---

5 Pour sauce onto four warm plates. Place the 'mosaics' on top and
   decorate.

Knot of Salmon
surrounding a Spinach and Dill Mousse with a Pumpkin Sauce

MAIN INGREDIENTS

¾lb salmon fillet, skinned
juice of ½ lemon
4 squares aluminium foil, buttered
6 Tbsp spinach and dill mousse,
    page 147
salt and white pepper

SAUCE

1½c warm pumpkin sauce, *page 145*

PRESENTATION

1 radish, sliced
8 asparagus tips
1 zucchini, blanched and sliced
4 broccoli florets, blanched
4 snow peas, blanched
4 cucumber 'barrels' *page 151*
    blanched
¼ stick (2 Tbsp) unsalted butter,
    clarified (optional)

---

1 Cut the salmon fillet into four equal portions lengthwise. Trim off any dark flesh.

---

2 Tie each strip of fillet into a loose knot; salmon is very flexible. Season with salt, pepper and lemon juice, and place on buttered foil squares.

---

3 Using a piping bag fitted with a star-shaped nozzle, pipe the spinach and dill mousse into the hole. Decorate the mousse with slices of radish and half an asparagus tip.

---

4 Steam the fish for about 8 minutes or until the mousse is thoroughly cooked. For the last minute of the steaming add the seasoned vegetables, or alternatively toss them in butter until they are warmed through, and drain carefully.

---

5 Divide the sauce equally between four warm plates. Carefully lift the salmon off the foil sheets onto the plates. Decorate with the warm vegetables.

Lobster and Scallops
with a Minted Orange Sauce

MAIN INGREDIENTS
1lb live lobster
6 scallops with coral, shelled and
    cleaned
$\frac{1}{4}$ stick (2 Tbsp) unsalted butter,
    clarified
salt and black pepper

SAUCE
1$\frac{1}{2}$c warm minted orange sauce,
    page 145

PRESENTATION
4 slices truffle
2 Tbsp julienned mint
1 orange, peeled and segmented

1 Cook the lobster 30 minutes in advance, in a boiling court-bouillon,
   for 10 minutes. Leave it in the cooking liquid. When it is cool
   enough to handle, shell it, removing the tail in one piece, and divide
   into two. Shell the claws. Keep warm.

2 Cut each scallop in half horizontally, with its coral.

3 Lightly sauté the scallops and corals for 20 seconds on each side in
   the clarified butter. Season, drain and keep warm.

4 Divide the sauce between four warm plates. Distribute the scallops
   (twelve halves) and lobster (two pieces of tail meat and two claws)
   between the plates and decorate with truffle, mint and orange.

*The orange and mint create an exciting taste for shellfish. Try the dish from
time to time with a saffron and ginger sauce.*

FILLETS OF TURBOT
larded with Truffle and
Salmon with a White Truffle Sauce

MAIN INGREDIENTS

2oz salmon fillet, skinned
1 small [1oz] truffle, cut into strips
$4 \times \frac{1}{4}$lb turbot fillets, skinned
$\frac{1}{2}$ stick (4 Tbsp) unsalted butter,
  clarified
1lb fresh spinach, blanched, central
  rib removed
salt and white pepper

SAUCE

$1\frac{1}{2}$c warm white truffle sauce, *page
  148*

---

1 Cut the salmon into strips the same size as the truffle.

---

2 Using a larding needle, thread the salmon and truffle through the turbot.

---

3 Slice each turbot fillet into three steaks. Season and steam for approximately 3 minutes.

---

4 Heat the butter. Toss the spinach in the butter until warmed through. Season well, and drain.

---

5 Divide the spinach between four warm plates. Arrange three pieces of turbot on each plate in a triangle, and pour a little warm sauce into the middle of each triangle. Serve the remainder of the sauce separately.

Exciting combinations can be developed by larding the turbot with other products – for example, anchovy and asparagus, or pimento and apple.

Spinach-Suited Langostino
with a Cucumber and Mint Sauce

MAIN INGREDIENTS

24 medium-sized langostino tails,
   cooked and shelled
24 leaves of fresh spinach,
   blanched, central rib removed

SAUCE

$1\frac{1}{2}$c warm cucumber and mint
   sauce, *page 142*

PRESENTATION

24 cucumber balls, made with the
   smallest parisienne cutter and
   blanched
24 tiny sprigs of mint

---

1 Wrap each langostino tail in a spinach leaf, leaving a small piece of tail showing.

---

2 Steam the langostino tails and the cucumber balls for 2 minutes.

---

3 Place an equal amount of warm sauce on four warm plates. Put six langostino tails on each plate, and decorate with cucumber and mint.

Zucchini can be used instead of cucumber, and the dish can be varied by having a selection of shellfish wrapped in spinach.

Feuilleté of White Crabmeat with Broccoli, Artichoke and Tomato on a Crab and Armagnac Sauce

MAIN INGREDIENTS

½ stick (4 Tbsp) unsalted butter, clarified
1 shallot, chopped
½ clove garlic, chopped
1 scallion, chopped
½ tsp chopped fresh ginger
white crab meat from 3lb cooked crab: use brown meat for sauce
4 triangles puff pastry approximately 2 inches along each side, cooked
salt and white pepper

SAUCE

1½ c warm crab and armagnac sauce, *page 141*.
2 tomatoes, peeled, seeded and diced
2 artichoke hearts, cooked and diced

PRESENTATION

broccoli florets, blanched

---

1 Heat half the butter in a pan and gently sweat the shallot, garlic, scallion and ginger until soft but not brown. Add the crab meat and heat until warmed through. Season.

---

2 Add the diced tomato and artichoke hearts to the sauce. Heat through.

---

3 Toss the broccoli in the remaining butter until warmed through. Season.

---

4 Reheat the pastry triangles in a hot oven for 2 minutes. Split them in two horizontally.

---

5 Divide the warm sauce equally between four warm plates. Place the bottom half of the pastry in the center of the plate, and arrange the crab on top. Top with pastry lids and decorate with broccoli.

I rarely advocate frozen foods, but there are several excellent brands of frozen crab meat which would turn this into a quick supper dish.

Galaxy of Seasonal Seafood
with a Champagne and Cucumber Sauce

MAIN INGREDIENTS

$\frac{1}{4}$lb salmon fillet, skinned and cut
    into 4 cubes
$\frac{1}{4}$lb turbot fillet, skinned and cut
    into 4 equal pieces
$\frac{1}{2}$lb lobster meat, cooked and sliced
    into 4 medallions
4 scallops with coral, shelled and
    washed
4 langostinos, cooked and shelled
4 mussels, cooked and shelled
juice of $\frac{1}{2}$ lemon
salt and white pepper

SAUCE

$1\frac{1}{2}$c warm champagne and
    cucumber sauce, *page 140*

PRESENTATION

2 tomatoes, peeled, seeded and
    quartered
12 cucumber 'barrels', *page 151*
24 cucumber balls

---

1 Either steam or gently poach the salmon and turbot and cucumber
'barrels' for 2 minutes. Add the other fish and cucumber balls, and
cook for a further 2 minutes. Season with salt, pepper and lemon
juice.

---

2 Arrange equal amounts of warm sauce on four warm plates. Top
with the fish and decorate.

---

*Use whatever shellfish appeals to you – few households will be able to find
just four slices of lobster or four mussels.*

Fillet of Brill with Lobster and a Lobster and Spinach Mousse served on a Chervil Sauce

MAIN INGREDIENTS

4 × 3oz brill fillets, skinned
juice of $\frac{1}{2}$ lemon
8 large spinach leaves, blanched, central rib removed
4 Tbsp lobster and spinach mousse, *page 144*
raw tail meat from $1\frac{1}{2}$ lb lobster: use claws and head for mousse
salt and white pepper

SAUCE

$1\frac{1}{2}$c warm dry vermouth and chervil sauce, *page 142*
2 tomatoes, peeled, seeded and diced

PRESENTATION

4 sprigs of chervil

---

1 Season the fillets with salt, pepper and lemon juice.

---

2 Wrap each brill fillet in two blanched spinach leaves. Make a deep incision through the spinach and into the fish. Pipe the lobster and spinach mousse into the incision.

---

3 Cut the lobster tail into twelve small medallions.

---

4 Steam the brill parcels for 6 minutes. Insert three pieces of lobster into the half-cooked mousse in each fillet. Steam for a further 4 minutes.

---

5 Add diced tomato to the sauce. Warm through.

---

6 Divide the sauce between four warm plates. Place a brill parcel on each plate. Decorate with chervil sprigs.

Fillets of white fish such as brill and turbot make excellent containers for mousses and other fillings.

Fricassée of Monkfish, Mussels and Vegetables with a Tomato and Rosemary Sauce

MAIN INGREDIENTS

$\frac{1}{2}$ lb monkfish fillet, skinned, cut into $\frac{1}{2}$ inch cubes

juice of $\frac{1}{2}$ lemon

$1\frac{1}{2}$ lb mussels, cooked and shelled: reserve juices for sauce

$1\frac{1}{2}$ lb vegetables, blanched: choose from snow peas, broccoli florets, asparagus tips, green beans

salt and white pepper

SAUCES

1 c warm rosemary sauce, *page 146*

$\frac{3}{4}$ c warm tomato and rosemary sauce, *page 147*

PRESENTATION

sprigs of chervil

1 tsp finely diced truffle

---

1 Season monkfish cubes with salt, pepper and lemon juice. Steam for about 6 minutes.

---

2 Add the mussels, vegetables and monkfish to the rosemary sauce. Warm through. Season.

---

3 Pour a ring of tomato and rosemary sauce round the edge of four warm plates. Divide the fricassée equally and spoon it onto the middle of each plate. Decorate.

A good dish, less expensive to make than most. You could substitute flakes of cod or haddock for the monkfish.

Trio of Vegetable Packets
enclosing Oysters, Scallops and Langostino with a Saffron and Ginger Sauce

MAIN INGREDIENTS

2 leeks, blanched
4 oysters, shelled
½ stick (4 Tbsp) unsalted butter, clarified
4 langostino tails, cooked and shelled
4 scallops, shelled and washed
4 Savoy cabbage leaves, blanched, central rib removed
¾c hot scallop mousse, *page 146*
4 spinach leaves, blanched, central rib removed
salt and white pepper

SAUCE

1½c warm saffron and ginger sauce, *page 146*, with finely chopped chives added

PRESENTATION

saffron stamens, soaked in warm water
whole chives

1 Split the leeks in two lengthwise and select eight of the larger outside leaves. Dry them and set aside. (Use the remainder for another recipe.)

2 Sauté the oysters for 20 seconds each side in warm butter. Season. Remove and drain on paper towels. Cook the langostino tails and scallops for the same length of time, but at a slightly higher temperature to give them a little color. Season and drain them.

3 Wrap each langostino tail in a cabbage leaf together with a tablespoon of scallop mousse. Wrap the scallops in spinach leaves, again with a tablespoon of mousse. Place a tablespoon of mousse in the center of each of four of the leek leaves, and top with oysters. Cover each oyster with a second leek leaf placed at right angles to the first leaf and tucked underneath. Trim the leek leaves if too long.

4 Steam the packages for about 8 minutes, or cook for a similar time in a medium oven in a little white wine or fish stock.

5 Divide the sauce between four warm plates and place the parcels on top. Decorate with saffron and chives.

Blanched lettuce leaves would also make good parcels.

MAGRET of DUCK WITH FIGS
on a Sauce enriched with a Fig Coulis

MAIN INGREDIENTS

1 duck magret (or 2 breasts of Long
   Island duckling)

SAUCE

2 Tbsp raspberry vinegar
1½c duck stock, *page 142*
1c fig coulis, *page 142*
½ stick (4 Tbsp) cold unsalted
   butter, diced
salt and black pepper

PRESENTATION

4 fresh figs
2 oranges, peeled and segmented

---

1 Place the duck skin side down in a frying pan with no fat or oil. Cook over a moderate heat until skin crisps and most of the natural fats have come out. Drain off the fat. Turn the duck over and cook for a further 3 minutes. The meat should be pink when cut. (The duck can be broiled or grilled if preferred.)

---

2 Remove the duck from pan and keep warm. Deglaze the pan with vinegar and add the duck stock. Boil to reduce by half. Add fig coulis and again boil to reduce until approximately 1½ cups. Strain the sauce and return to pan. Add the cold butter piece by piece. Season.

---

3 Put the figs into a medium oven to warm through for 5 minutes. Take them out and cut into six sections through the stem, but leave the sections attached to the base.

---

4 Thinly slice the duck breasts. Arrange equal amounts of sauce on four warm plates. Put the duck fillets on top and decorate.

Boned Quail in Pastry
filled with a Game Mousse and served with a Port and Orange Sauce

MAIN INGREDIENTS

4 quail, boned
$\frac{1}{2}$ stick (4 Tbsp) unsalted butter,
    clarified
4 circular croûtons, 2 inches
    diameter, cut from slices of white
    bread
4 sheets filo pastry
$\frac{1}{4}$c game mousse, *page 142*
4 grapes, peeled and seeded
salt and black pepper

SAUCE

$1\frac{1}{2}$c warm port and orange sauce,
    page 145

PRESENTATION

1 leek, julienned and blanched,
    warmed in butter before serving
1 orange, peeled and segmented
8 grapes, peeled, halved and seeded

1   Fry the quail in half the butter on all sides until the skin is brown.
    Season. Remove from pan and cut each one in half along the length
    of the breast.

2   Fry the croûtons in the same pan until golden on both sides.

3   Brush both sides of each sheet of pastry with the remaining clarified
    butter. Fold in half.

4   Place a fried croûton in the middle of each sheet of pastry. Divide the
    game mousse equally between the croûtons, shape into a mound
    and top with a grape. Surround this with the quail halves. Gather
    the four corners of the pastry, and pinch and twist to make a parcel,
    as in the diagrams on *page 138*. Roast in a medium oven for 20
    minutes, covering the top with foil if they become too brown. Drain
    the quail parcels on paper towels. Arrange on warm plates with the
    sauce and decorate.

MEDALLION OF VENISON WITH OYSTER MUSHROOMS on a Garlic Cream and a Gin and Juniper Sauce

MAIN INGREDIENTS

4 × 1oz slices fresh duck foie gras
$\frac{1}{4}$ stick (2 Tbsp) unsalted butter, clarified
4 × 4oz medallions of saddle venison, previously marinated, *page 144*
8 oyster mushrooms, washed and dried
4 Tbsp game mousse, preferably venison, *page 142*
4 thin slices truffle
24 chervil sprigs
4 squares caul fat
salt and black pepper

SAUCES

$\frac{3}{4}$c warm gin and juniper sauce, *page 143*: made using the marinade
$\frac{3}{4}$c cold garlic cream, *page 143*

PRESENTATION

1 tsp finely diced truffle
$\frac{1}{4}$lb fresh duck foie gras, sautéed and diced

---

1 Sauté the foie gras slices for 15 seconds each side (no extra fat is needed). Season. Allow to cool on paper towels so that excess fat is absorbed.

---

2 Add the butter to the same pan. Fry the venison medallions on both sides until brown, approximately 30 seconds on each side. Season and remove. Add the oyster mushrooms, Sauté for 1 minute each side and season.

---

3 When all these ingredients are cold, place the four venison medallions on a flat surface. Put a piece of foie gras on top of the medallion and a spoonful of mousse on the foie gras. Smooth with a palette knife. On top of the mousse place an oyster mushroom, truffle slice and chervil sprigs, and wrap the whole parcel in the caul fat. Cook in a medium oven for 8 to 10 minutes. For the last 2 minutes of cooking add the remaining four oyster mushrooms to warm through.

---

4 Spoon the gin and juniper sauce over half of each plate and the garlic cream over the other half. The two sauces will remain separate. Place an oyster mushroom and a medallion in the middle. Decorate with diced truffle and foie gras.

Venison is becoming more popular as the growth in deer-farming makes it more available and less expensive.

Saddle of Hare with Prunes and a Celeriac Mousse, served on a Horseradish and Onion Sauce

MAIN INGREDIENTS

1 saddle of hare, sinews removed
cooked marinade, *page 144*
$\frac{3}{4}$c celery root mousse, *page 140*
$\frac{1}{2}$ stick (4 Tbsp) unsalted butter,
   clarified
$\frac{1}{2}$ stick (4 Tbsp) cold unsalted
   butter, diced
salt and black pepper

SAUCE

1c warm horseradish and onion
   sauce, *page 143*

PRESENTATION

12 prunes, stoned
4 Tbsp brandy
4 Tbsp cold tea

---

1 Twenty-four hours in advance, marinate the hare in cooked marinade. Soak the prunes in brandy and tea.

---

2 Butter the inside of four ramekins and fill with celery root mousse. Smooth the top and tap the dishes on a hard surface to remove any air bubbles. Place in a roasting pan half full of warm water. Cook in a medium oven for about 12 to 15 minutes. Test by inserting the tip of a knife or skewer into the mousse: if it comes out clean the mousse is cooked.

---

3 Remove the meat from the marinade, reserving the marinade. Roast the meat in a hot oven for 12 minutes, basting occasionally with the remaining clarified butter.

---

4 Simmer the prunes in their liquid for 15 minutes. Strain and add the juice to the meat marinade. Boil to reduce by half. Season. Add the cold butter pieces, stirring until emulsified. Halve four of the prunes and dice the rest.

---

5 Remove the meat from the saddle and slice it into thin strips.

---

6 Turn the mousses out onto four plates and top with diced prunes. Arrange meat, prune halves and sauces around them.

Venison or rabbit can be used as a substitute for hare. Try with a Jerusalem artichoke mousse for a change.

Tenderloin of Beef with fresh Duck Foie Gras and two Truffle Sauces

MAIN INGREDIENTS

$\frac{1}{4}$ stick (2 Tbsp) unsalted butter,
    clarified
4 × 3oz pieces of beef tenderloin
4 × 1oz slices fresh duck foie gras
salt and black pepper

SAUCES

$\frac{3}{4}$c warm dark truffle sauce, *page*
    147
$\frac{3}{4}$c warm white truffle sauce, *page*
    148

PRESENTATION

2 slices truffle, julienned
1 orange, peeled and segmented
8 sprigs of chervil

---

1 Heat the butter in a pan. Sauté the beef tenderloin pieces for approximately 3 minutes on each side. Season. Remove from pan and keep them warm.

---

2 In a hot clean pan sauté the foie gras slices for 20 seconds on each side (no extra fat is needed). Season. Place a piece of foie gras on top of each piece of beef tenderloin.

---

3 Deglaze the pan with the dark truffle sauce and stir.

---

4 Divide the sauces between four warm plates, pouring the white truffle sauce around the edge of the plate and the dark sauce in the center. Place one piece of beef tenderloin topped with foie gras in the middle of each plate and decorate.

An expensive but pleasing dish. If you need a substitute for the foie gras, try chicken liver or calf's liver.

Calf's Sweetbreads, Liver and Kidney served with Ogen Melon and Saffron Sauce

MAIN INGREDIENTS

4 × 1½oz slices Dutch calf's liver
1 small calf's sweetbread, cooked
  and cut into 4 slices
1 small calf's kidney, without suet,
  soaked in milk for 30 minutes
¼ stick (2 Tbsp) unsalted butter,
  clarified
1 Tbsp cooking oil
salt and white pepper

SAUCE

1½c warm saffron and ginger sauce,
  page 146

PRESENTATION

1 small Ogen melon, scooped into
  balls with medium parisienne
  cutter
4 cherry tomatoes, peeled, seeded
  and quartered

---

1 Season the liver and sweetbread.

---

2 Remove the kidney from the milk and cut it in half lengthwise. Remove the core. Halve each piece again. Season and set aside.

---

3 Heat half the butter and the oil in a frying pan. Add the kidney and liver to the hot fat, browning both sides. Add the sweetbreads and brown. Sauté until the liver and kidney are sufficiently cooked. Drain meats in paper towels.

---

4 Sauté the melon lightly in the remaining butter.

---

5 Divide the sauce between four warm plates. Place the meat and melon balls on the sauce and decorate.

Offal in most forms is regaining its popularity. Beautiful textures combined with the unusual flavor of a saffron sauce make this dish memorable.

Ballotine of Baby Chicken with Crab, Cucumber and Ginger on a Tomato and Garlic Sauce

MAIN INGREDIENTS

$\frac{1}{4}$ cucumber, peeled, seeded and
  finely diced
1 tsp finely chopped fresh ginger
$\frac{3}{4}$c dry white wine
4 baby chicken legs, boned: see
  diagram, *page 139*
4 Tbsp hot scallop mousse, *page
  146*
6oz white crab meat
4 squares caul fat
$\frac{1}{4}$ stick (2 Tbsp) unsalted butter,
  clarified
salt and white pepper

SAUCE

$1\frac{1}{2}$c warm tomato and garlic sauce,
  page 147

PRESENTATION

$\frac{1}{2}$ cucumber, peeled, cut into $\frac{1}{2}$ inch
  slices, centers removed to make
  rings: reserve peel
1 tomato, peeled, seeded and finely
  chopped
cucumber peel, julienned
1 tsp chopped chives

---

1 Earlier in the day, salt the diced cucumber and cucumber rings.
  Leave for 30 minutes, then drain and rinse to remove excess salt.
  Blanch the cucumber rings for 3 minutes, the diced cucumber and
  peel for 1 minute and the ginger for 1 minute in the dry white wine.
  Drain and set aside to cool. (Use the wine for the sauce.)

---

2 Season the inside of the chicken legs.

---

3 Mix the mousse, crab meat, diced cucumber and ginger thoroughly.

---

4 Using a small spoon or a piping bag fill the chicken legs with the
  crab mixture. Fold the caul fat over the legs, sealing in the crab. (See
  diagram on *page 139*.) Fill the cucumber rings with chopped
  tomato. Steam the chicken legs for approximately 12 to 15 minutes.
  For the last 2 minutes place the cucumber rings in the steamer to
  warm through. Remove the legs from the steamer, and sauté gently
  in butter, skin side first, until golden brown. Drain.

---

5 Divide the sauce between four warm plates. Place the chicken on
  the sauce. Add three cucumber rings and some julienned cucumber
  peel to each plate. Decorate.

FEUILLETÉ OF PARTRIDGE AND MANGO
with a Spinach Sauce and a Mango Coulis

MAIN INGREDIENTS

2 oven-ready partridges
2 pieces Canadian bacon
$\frac{1}{2}$ stick (4 Tbsp) unsalted butter,
   clarified
1 shallot, chopped
1 clove garlic, chopped
8 puff pastry crescents, cooked and
   halved horizontally
salt and black pepper

SAUCES

$\frac{3}{4}$c warm spinach sauce, *page 147*
$\frac{3}{4}$c warm mango coulis, *page 144*

PRESENTATION

1 mango, peeled and flesh julienned
tiny rolls of blanched spinach
   leaves

---

1 Season the partridges. Place bacon over the breasts and tie with string. Roast for 10 minutes in a hot oven.

---

2 Remove the bacon, breasts and legs. Lower the temperature and return the breasts to the oven for 8 minutes. Skin the legs and cut off the meat. Chop finely.

---

3 Sweat the chopped shallot and garlic in butter until soft, and add the chopped partridge legs. Season.

---

4 Remove the partridge breasts from oven and put the pastry cases into the oven for 2 minutes to warm through. Slice the breasts thinly.

---

5 Place a spoonful of mango coulis in the center of four warm plates and pour the spinach sauce round the edge of the plate. Put the bottom halves of the pastry crescents on top of the mango coulis and place a spoonful of the diced leg between the crescents. Arrange the strips of partridge around the edge of the pastry bottoms, put on the pastry lids and top with mango julienne. Decorate with sliced spinach rolls.

Beef and Veal Burgers with Oysters and Spinach

MAIN INGREDIENTS

1 shallot, finely chopped

$\frac{1}{2}$ stick (4 Tbsp) unsalted butter, clarified

8 oysters, shelled and finely chopped: reserve sieved juices for oyster cream

2 Tbsp light cream mixed with 1 egg yolk

8 leaves spinach, blanched, central rib removed

$\frac{1}{2}$lb each tenderloin veal and beef trimmings, finely chopped

8 squares caul fat

salt and black pepper

SAUCES

$\frac{1}{4}$lb bone marrow, poached and diced

$\frac{3}{4}$c warm red burgundy sauce, *page 146*

$\frac{3}{4}$c warm oyster and champagne sauce, *page 145*

PRESENTATION

1 tomato, peeled, seeded and julienned

cucumber peel, blanched and julienned

$\frac{1}{4}$lb bone marrow, poached and diced

---

1 Sweat the shallot in half the butter, add the chopped oysters and cook for 30 seconds over high heat. Season with ground black pepper. Drain any juices that may have been released by the cooking and use these for the sauce. Add the cream and egg yolk mixture. Cook for 1 minute without boiling. Allow to cool.

---

2 Spread the spinach leaves on a flat surface, season, and place a teaspoon of the cold oyster mixture on each leaf. Wrap up.

---

3 Divide both the veal and beef into four equal amounts. Season well. Shape each into a 'burger'; make an indentation in the center of each in which to place an oyster parcel. Mold the meat around the parcel to cover it completely. Wrap each 'burger' in caul fat. Sauté them in the remaining butter to brown all sides, then put them in a medium oven for 5 to 8 minutes.

---

4 Add the diced marrow to the burgundy sauce. Heat through.

---

5 Place two spoonfuls of oyster and champagne sauce on each of four warm plates. Spoon the burgundy sauce around this; the two sauces will remain separate. Place a veal burger and a beef burger on each circle of oyster and champagne sauce. Decorate.

A good way of using expensive trimmings. The dish also works well with finely chopped fish – monkfish proving to be the best.

Flowering Zucchini with a pastrycase of Asparagus and buttered Chanterelles

MAIN INGREDIENTS

4 small zucchini with flowers attached

6 Tbsp wild mushroom mousse, *page 149*

4 round pie dough tartlet cases, cooked

4 Tbsp tomato coulis, *page 147*

8 asparagus tips, blanched

$2\frac{1}{2}$c chanterelles, washed and dried

$\frac{1}{2}$ stick (4 Tbsp) unsalted butter, clarified

1 clove garlic, finely chopped

1 shallot, finely chopped

salt and black pepper

SAUCE

$1\frac{1}{2}$c warm wild mushroom sauce, *page 149*

PRESENTATION

1 leek, julienned and blanched

1 tomato, peeled, seeded and julienned

1 tsp chopped chives

---

1 Wash the zucchini flowers carefully without soaking to remove any insects. Using a small piping bag, fill the flowers with wild mushroom mousse. Fold the petals inwards to enclose the mousse. Steam for approximately 8 to 10 minutes until the mousse is cooked. Make several cuts lengthwise along the zucchini to within $\frac{1}{2}$ inch of the flower and fan it out, Keep warm.

---

2 Fill the four pastry tartlets with tomato coulis and top with seasoned, buttered asparagus tips. Place in a warm oven to heat through.

---

3 Sauté the chanterelles in the rest of the butter, with the garlic and the shallot. Season.

---

4 Spoon the sauce onto four warm plates. Arrange some mushrooms, a zucchini and a tartlet on each plate. Decorate.

Lamb Sirloin
with an Eggplant Mousse and a Tomato and Garlic Sauce

MAIN INGREDIENTS

3 bulbs of garlic, separated into
   cloves and peeled
$1\frac{1}{4}$c goose fat
$\frac{3}{4}$c eggplant mousse, *page 142*
lamb sirloin (approx. 1lb)
$\frac{1}{4}$ stick (2 Tbsp) unsalted butter,
   clarified
4 Tbsp tomato concassé, *page 147*
salt and black pepper

SAUCE

$1\frac{1}{2}$c warm tomato and garlic sauce,
   page 147

PRESENTATION

1 small bunch of chives, whole

---

1 Cook the garlic cloves slowly in goose fat for about 1 hour. Allow to cool in goose fat.

---

2 Butter four individual tartlet molds and fill with eggplant mousse. Cover with sheets of buttered wax paper. Cook in a bain-marie in a medium oven for approximately 10 to 14 minutes.

---

3 Brown the lamb all over in clarified butter. Season. Remove the mousses from the oven. Increase the temperature and roast the lamb in the oven for 8 to 12 minutes. Turn the oven off, leaving the lamb inside, and return the mousses to keep warm.

---

4 Heat the tomato concassé. Warm the garlic cloves in the goose fat and drain. Cut the lamb into about twenty thin slices. Turn the eggplant mousses out onto four warm plates, top with tomato concassé and lamb. Spoon the sauce around the mousses. Decorate with garlic cloves and chives.

FEUILLETÉ OF MORELS AND ASPARAGUS
with a Wild Mushroom Sauce

MAIN INGREDIENTS

8 small puff pastry crescents,
  cooked
½ stick (4 Tbsp) unsalted butter,
  clarified
1c fresh morels, thoroughly
  washed and halved
28 asparagus tips, cooked
salt and white pepper

SAUCE

1½c warm wild mushroom sauce,
  page 149

PRESENTATION

4 sprigs of chervil

---

1 Split the pastry crescents horizontally. Put them in a warm oven for
  3 minutes to heat through.

---

2 Heat the butter in a frying pan. When hot, add the morels. Fry for 3
  minutes, stirring occasionally.

---

3 Turn down the heat and add the asparagus tips to the frying pan.
  Cook for a further 2 minutes, turning regularly. Season. Drain off
  excess butter.

---

4 Divide the sauce between four warm plates. Put the bottoms of the
  pastry crescents in the center. Arrange the asparagus and morels,
  and put the tops on the pastry crescents.

Veal Tenderloin
with Citrus Fruits on Caviar and a Champagne Sauce

MAIN INGREDIENTS

$4 \times \frac{1}{4}$lb pieces veal tenderloin, sinews removed
$\frac{1}{4}$ stick (2 Tbsp) unsalted butter, clarified
1 Tbsp oil
salt and black pepper

SAUCE

$1\frac{1}{2}$c warm champagne sauce, *page 140*
1oz caviar

PRESENTATION

cucumber peel, julienned and blanched
citrus fruits, peeled and segmented with the peel, julienned and blanched: choose from lemon, grapefruit, lime and orange

1 Season the veal with salt and black pepper. Put the butter in a frying pan, add the oil and when hot cook for 2 to 3 minutes on each side. Drain on paper towels.

2 Add the caviar to the warm sauce just before serving. Divide the sauce between four warm plates, place a veal fillet on each plate and decorate.

Do not use lumpfish roe as a substitute for the caviar – the taste would be too strong.

FEUILLÉTÉ of WOODCOCK AND FOIE GRAS
on a Port and Cranberry Sauce

MAIN INGREDIENTS

2 woodcock, plucked, but not
  drawn
2 pieces of Canadian bacon
½ stick (4 Tbsp) unsalted butter,
  clarified
1 shallot, chopped
1 clove garlic, chopped
6oz fresh foie gras, diced
1 Tbsp port
4 puff pastry circles, cooked and
  halved horizontally
salt and black pepper

SAUCE

1½c warm port and cranberry
  sauce, *page 145*

PRESENTATION

4 broccoli florets, blanched
1⅓c cranberries, blanched

1 Truss each woodcock with its own beak through the thighs and
  remove the eyes. Season. Place bacon over the breasts and tie with
  string. Roast for 12 to 15 minutes in a hot oven with half the butter,
  basting regularly. Remove the bacon, cut away legs, breasts and
  heads, and keep warm. Remove the entrails from the carcasses with
  a small spoon, discarding the gizzards. Chop the entrails.

2 Sauté the shallot and garlic in the remaining butter. Cook over a
  low heat to soften, then add the diced foie gras and entrails. Raise
  the heat and sautè quickly. Season and sprinkle with port. Drain and
  keep warm. Loosen the juices in the pan with the sauce and stir to
  combine.

3 Spread the bottom halves of the pastry cases with foie gras mixture.
  Heat the pastry cases in a warm oven for 2 minutes.

4 Split the heads in two through the beak.

5 Carve the breasts. Toss the broccoli in butter to warm. Season.
  Divide the sauce between four warm plates. Place the bottom half
  of the pastry case on the sauce, and arrange the slices of breast
  around the pastry base. Set the pastry lid on top. Arrange a leg and
  half a head on the plate with a few cranberries and the broccoli.

*Woodcock is my favorite game bird, but snipe or wild duck make good
substitutes.*

VEAL TENDERLOIN WITH A 'SOUFFLÉ' and a delicate Rosemary Sauce

MAIN INGREDIENTS

$\frac{1}{4}$ stick (2 Tbsp) unsalted butter, clarified

4 × $\frac{1}{4}$lb veal tenderloin medallions

6 Tbsp chicken mousse, *page 141*; 2 extra egg whites whipped and folded in

$\frac{1}{4}$lb veal sweetbreads, diced

$\frac{1}{4}$lb duck foie gras, diced

$\frac{1}{4}$ sweet red bell pepper, roasted, peeled and julienned

$\frac{1}{4}$ sweet green bell pepper, roasted, peeled and julienned

1 slice truffle, julienned

4 pieces caul fat

salt and white pepper

SAUCE

1$\frac{1}{2}$c warm rosemary sauce, *page 146*

PRESENTATION

1 small cucumber

8 asparagus spears, blanched

1 carrot, peeled, cut into sticks and blanched

2 slices truffle, julienned

---

1 Heat half the butter in a frying pan. Brown the veal medallions on all sides, season, remove from the heat and allow to cool

---

2 Add the diced veal, sweetbreads and duck foie gras to the chicken mousse. Use a palette knife to smooth some mousse on top of each medallion. Decorate the top of the mousse with red and green pepper and truffle, as in the photograph. Wrap the medallions in the caul fat, completely enclosing the mousse. Place on a greased oven tray and put in a hot oven for 8 to 10 minutes.

---

3 Meanwhile, peel half the cucumber and, using a small parisienne cutter, shape into cucumber balls. Cut the unpeeled half into 'barrels', *page 151*. Blanch the balls in boiling salted water for 1 minute, and the 'barrels' for 3 minutes.

---

4 Toss all the vegetables in the remaining butter. Season well.

---

5 Divide the sauce between four warm plates. Drain the vegetables and arrange them around the plates. Place the veal medallions in the middle, and top the cucumber 'barrels' with the julienne of truffle.

Not a soufflé in the true sense of the word.

Mousse of Scallops
with Lamb Sirloin and Snow Peas
on a Tomato and Basil Sauce

MAIN INGREDIENTS

$\frac{3}{4}$ stick (6 Tbsp) unsalted butter,
  clarified
$\frac{3}{4}$c hot scallop mousse, *page 146*
1 lamb sirloin (approx. 1lb)

SAUCES

$\frac{3}{4}$c warm tomato and basil sauce,
  page 147
$\frac{3}{4}$c hollandaise sauce, *page 143*
6 Tbsp fish stock, *page 142*

PRESENTATION

1 shallot, chopped
4 scallops with coral, shelled and
  diced
$\frac{1}{4}$lb snow peas, blanched
1 tsp granulated sugar
1 slice truffle, finely diced
salt and white pepper

1 Butter the inside of four ramekins, and fill with scallop mousse.
Smooth the top and tap the dishes on a hard surface to remove any
air bubbles. Cover with buttered foil. Place in a bain-marie half full
of warm water. Cook in a medium oven for approximately 12 to 15
minutes. Test by inserting the tip of a knife or skewer into the
mousse: if it comes out clean the mousse is cooked. Remove them
from the oven and keep warm. Raise the oven temperature.

2 Fry the lamb on all sides in some of the butter to seal it. Season and
cook it in a hot oven for approximately 8 minutes.

3 Meanwhile, dilute the hollandaise with warm fish stock to a coating
consistency.

4 Sweat the shallot in remaining butter until soft but not brown. Add
the scallops and warm through. Season. Drain and keep warm. Toss
the snow peas in the same pan with the sugar. Season.

5 When the lamb is cooked, cut it into sixteen slices and keep warm.
Turn a mousse out onto each plate, absorbing excess liquid with
paper towels. Spoon a little hollandaise over each one, then pour
tomato and basil sauce around the edge. The sauce will remain
separate. Place lamb and snow peas around the plate. Top the
mousse with diced scallop and sprinkle with diced truffle.

Breast of Corn-fed Pigeon
stuffed with a Mousse of Pigeon and Garlic served with a Red Burgundy Sauce

MAIN INGREDIENTS

3 bulbs of garlic, separated into
   cloves and peeled
3 Tbsp goose fat
$\frac{3}{4}$c garlic cream, *page 143*
pigeon mousse using meat from
   pigeon legs and recipe for game
   mousse, *page 142* ($\frac{1}{2}$ quantity)
breasts from 2 corn-fed pigeons,
   boned
4 pieces caul fat
2 medium potatoes, peeled
salt and white pepper

SAUCES

$\frac{3}{4}$c warm champagne sauce, *page
   140*, with 2 Tbsp garlic cream,
   page 143, added
1c warm red burgundy sauce, *page
   146*

PRESENTATION

1 tomato, peeled, seeded and diced
1 tsp chopped chives

---

1   Boil the garlic in three changes of water for 5 minutes each time. Roast for 5 minutes in a medium oven with the goose fat.

---

2   Meanwhile, fold the garlic cream gently into the pigeon mousse. Make a deep cut in the side of each pigeon breast to form a pocket. Use a piping bag to fill the pocket with the pigeon and garlic mousse. Season. Wrap each breast in a piece of caul fat.

---

3   Wash and grate the potato. Heat four small all-metal frying pans or one larger one. Drain half the goose fat from the garlic, and put some into each pan. Place a small handful of grated potato in each hot frying pan, and press down with a palette knife to make a small potato cake. Brown on both sides, season and then put the pans in the oven for 10 to 12 minutes.

---

4   Put the pigeon breasts into the tray of garlic and roast for 8 to 12 minutes. The pigeon and potato should be ready at more or less the same time.

---

5   Slice each pigeon breast. Place a spoonful of champagne and garlic sauce in the center of four warm plates. Pour the burgundy sauce around the edge. Place a potato cake on top of the garlic sauce, and the sliced pigeon breast and garlic around the potato. Decorate.

'The Ultimate'
Whole Truffle en Croûte
with a Morel Sauce

MAIN INGREDIENTS

1 shallot, chopped
1 clove garlic, finely chopped
$\frac{1}{4}$ stick (2 Tbsp) unsalted butter,
  clarified
$\frac{1}{4}$lb fresh duck foie gras, finely diced
$\frac{1}{4}$lb spinach, cooked and finely
  chopped
4 slices Parma ham
4 truffles, approximately $1\frac{1}{2}$oz each,
  cooked
4 sheets filo pastry, buttered on
  both sides
salt and black pepper

SAUCE

$1\frac{1}{2}$c warm morel sauce, *page 145*

PRESENTATION

truffle slices, julienned
4 Tbsp meat stock, boiled down to a
  full glaze

---

1 Sweat the shallot and garlic in the butter, add the foie gras, cook for
   30 seconds and then add the chopped spinach. Mix well to absorb
   all the fats. Season with salt and black pepper. Allow to cool.

---

2 Spread out four slices of Parma ham on a flat surface. Place a
   spoonful of spinach mixture on each piece of ham, and then a
   truffle. Wrap into a bundle, and enclose this in filo pastry: see the
   diagram on *page 138*.

---

3 Bake in a medium hot oven for 10 minutes or until golden brown.

---

4 Divide the morel sauce between four warm plates. Place a cooked
   pastry parcel in the center, and decorate with the truffle julienne
   and drops of meat glaze.

Diagrams by David Gifford

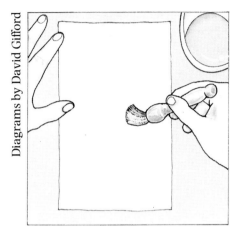

1 Brush filo on both sides with melted butter

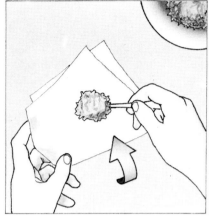

2 Fold sheet in half and place spoonful of filling in the center.

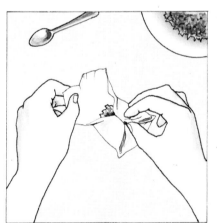

3 Bring corners together.

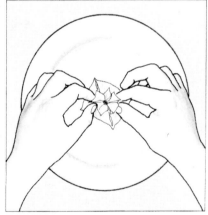

4 Pinch and twist pastry together at the top to seal the parcel. Stand on floured plate in refrigerator until ready to use.

BONING AND STUFFING A CHICKEN LEG

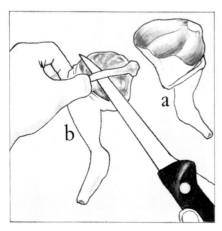

1 **a** Pull skin away from flesh to avoid piercing it while boning the leg.
b With leg other way up, make an incision along the flesh directly above the bone. Ease flesh off the bone; it should come away cleanly.

2 Cut around joint, then continue down second piece of bone with a scraping action. Once flesh has been cleared low enough, snap off bone at end knuckle. Trim off piece of scaly 'ankle' to leave small protrusion of bone.

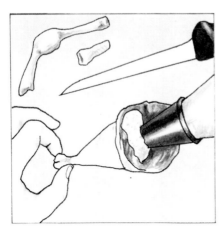

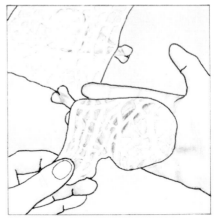

3 Pull skin back over flesh and, using piping bag, fill leg with mousse.

4 Wrap leg securely in caul fat to ensure it holds its shape.

SAUCES, MOUSSES, FILLINGS, DRESSINGS, STOCKS AND MARINADES

STOCKS Well made stocks are vital in good cooking, providing a basis for superb sauces. Make them whenever you have a little time to spare, and freeze them in small pots; or freeze in ice cube trays and turn the cubes out into labelled plastic bags. Keep pan uncovered throughout cooking. Use stock cubes only in emergencies. Meat, poultry or fish stocks can be further reduced to make a demi-glaze or jelly (reduce by $\frac{1}{2}$) or a full glaze or extract (reduce by $\frac{3}{4}$); see also *page 148*. This can't be done with vegetable stock; nor with stock cubes, which would merely become more concentrated.

SAUCES When the type of stock is not specified, use a stock based on the main ingredient of the dish which the sauce accompanies (e.g. for a chicken dish, use chicken stock in sauce, etc.). Most of the sauces can be used cold: adapt the recipe simply by leaving out the addition of cold butter at the end and by thinning the sauce, if necessary, with stock. Unless otherwise specified, recipes make approx. $1\frac{1}{2}$ cups.

AVOCADO AND BASIL SHERBET
2 ripe avocados, pitted and peeled/juice of 1 lemon/$\frac{1}{3}$c sugar/2c water/salt/2 Tbsp basil sauce (*pesto, page 150*)/2 Tbsp chopped basil leaves
Purée avocados with lemon juice. Dissolve sugar in water. Add salt, basil sauce and basil. Blend all ingredients in food processor until smooth. Put in ice cream maker or in tub in freezer. If in tub, stir when starting to freeze, and replace in freezer. (Makes approx. 3c.)

BROCCOLI SAUCE
1 shallot, chopped/1 clove garlic, chopped/ sprig of rosemary/pinch of grated nutmeg/ chopped stalks from 6 large heads broccoli/ $\frac{1}{2}$c Alsatian wine/1 bay leaf/$1\frac{1}{4}$c vegetable stock/florets from broccoli/$\frac{1}{2}$c 2 Tbsp heavy cream/$\frac{1}{4}$ stick (2 Tbsp) cold unsalted butter/ salt and white pepper/squeeze of lemon juice
Add first 7 ingredients to stock. Bring to a boil. Reduce by $\frac{1}{2}$. Strain through fine sieve. In separate pan of boiling salted water, cook broccoli florets for 7 minutes. Drain. Add to stock. Add cream. Liquidize. Reheat gently. Skim.

Add butter in small pieces. Season. Add lemon juice.

CELERY ROOT MOUSSE, HOT
1 bulb celery root/1 shallot, finely chopped/$\frac{1}{4}$ stick (2 Tbsp) unsalted butter, clarified/2 sage leaves/2c vegetable stock (*page 148*)/$\frac{1}{4}$c cream/1 whole egg + 2 yolks/salt and white pepper/more butter for molds
Peel celery root. Cut into 1 inch cubes. Boil in plenty of water for 5 minutes. Drain. Sweat shallot in butter until soft but not colored. Add sage, celery root and vegetable stock. Bring to a boil. Simmer for 15 to 18 minutes or until celery root is tender. Drain and return liquid to heat. Boil until reduced to 2 Tbsp. Return celery root. Liquidize. Fold in cream, egg and yolks. Pass through fine sieve. Season. Butter molds. Fill with mixture. Cover tops with buttered wax paper. Cook in bain-marie in medium oven for 15 to 20 minutes or until firm. Test by inserting skewer; if it comes out clean, mousse is cooked. (Makes approx. $\frac{3}{4}$c.)

CHAMPAGNE AND BASIL SAUCE Use champagne sauce recipe (*below*). Replace thyme with 2 Tbsp basil sauce (*pesto, page 150*). Add julienned basil leaves with the cream.

CHAMPAGNE AND CUCUMBER SAUCE
$\frac{1}{2}$ cucumber, peeled, seeded and finely chopped/sprig of rosemary/1 shallot, chopped/$1\frac{1}{4}$c chicken stock (*opposite*)/1 glass champagne/$\frac{1}{2}$c 2 Tbsp heavy cream/$\frac{1}{4}$ stick (2 Tbsp) cold unsalted butter/salt and white pepper/1 Tbsp champagne vinegar
Add first 3 ingredients to stock. Bring to a boil. Reduce by $\frac{1}{2}$. Discard rosemary. Liquidize sauce. Pass through fine sieve. Add champagne. Bring to a boil. Simmer for 5 minutes. Add cream. Simmer for 5 minutes more. Add butter a small piece at a time. Season. Add vinegar.

CHAMPAGNE SAUCE
Sprig of thyme/1 shallot, chopped/pinch of grated nutmeg/1 glass champagne/$1\frac{1}{4}$c stock/$1\frac{1}{4}$c heavy cream/$\frac{1}{4}$ stick (2 Tbsp) cold unsalted butter/salt and white pepper/1 Tbsp champagne vinegar
Add first 4 ingredients to stock. Bring to a boil. Reduce by $\frac{3}{4}$. Strain through fine sieve. Add cream, Return to heat. Simmer for 5 minutes. Add butter a small piece at a time. Season. Stir in vinegar. For a fizzy effect proceed as above, reducing stock a little further.

Just before serving add $\frac{1}{4}$ glass extra champagne.

CHICKEN GLAZE Make chicken stock recipe (*below*) and reduce by $\frac{3}{4}$.

CHICKEN MOUSSE, HOT
1 shallot, finely chopped/$\frac{1}{8}$ stick (1 Tbsp) unsalted butter, clarified/1 Tbsp chicken glaze/meat from 2 large chicken breasts, skinned and boned/salt and white pepper/ $2\frac{1}{2}$c heavy cream/2 egg whites
Sweat shallot in butter. Add chicken glaze. Leave to cool. Add rest of ingredients as in game mousse recipe. Cook as in recipe or in bain-marie in a medium oven. (Makes approx. 1c.)

CHICKEN STOCK
2lb chicken carcasses and giblets (except liver), chopped/1 pig's trotter or calf's foot, chopped/2 whole onions, each stuck with 2 cloves/1 carrot, thinly sliced/2 cloves garlic, crushed/1 stick celery, sliced/whites of 2 leeks, sliced/1 bouquet garni/$\frac{1}{2}$ bottle dry white wine/1 tsp crushed white peppercorns
Put carcasses, giblets and trotter in water to cover. Bring to a boil. Skim. Add all other ingredients. Add $2\frac{1}{2}$ qt water. Bring to a boil. Simmer for 3 to 4 hours, skimming regularly and adding more water if needed. Strain through fine sieve lined with paper towel or wet cheesecloth. Leave to settle. Remove fat, skimming off last traces with paper towel. Return to heat. Reduce to $2\frac{1}{2}$ cups.

CHLOROPHYLL COLORING
A paste of puréed green leaves and herbs, used to improve color and flavor of green sauces and mousses.
2lb spinach/1 shallot, chopped/1 clove garlic, chopped/fresh herbs (chervil, chives, basil, tarragon, parsley), chopped/salt and white pepper
Put first 4 ingredients in blender with 5 cups water and blend slowly. Pour mixture through cheesecloth into pan. Squeeze out all liquid. Discard pulp. Set over medium heat, stirring constantly. It will coagulate into a green purée on top of the water: remove from heat at once. Don't let it boil. Season. Pour slowly into cheesecloth. Let liquid run away. Scrape purée from cheesecloth. Store in closed container in refrigerator. Use sparingly.

CRAB AND ARMAGNAC SAUCE
1 shallot, finely chopped/1 clove garlic, finely chopped/$\frac{1}{4}$ stick (2 Tbsp) unsalted butter, clarified/brown meat from 3lb cooked crab/1 tsp Dijon mustard/sprig of thyme/1 tsp tomato purée/2 Tbsp tomato concassé (see *page 147*)/pinch of grated nutmeg/1 glass dry white wine/2c fish stock (*page 142*)/$\frac{1}{2}$c (2 Tbsp) whipping cream/1 Tbsp port/2 Tbsp armagnac/$\frac{1}{4}$ stick (2 Tbsp) more cold unsalted butter/salt and white pepper/squeeze of lemon juice
Sweat shallot and garlic in clarified butter until soft but not brown. Add crab, mustard, thyme, tomato purée, tomato concassé, nutmeg, white wine and stock. Bring to a boil. Reduce by $\frac{1}{2}$. Discard thyme. Liquidize mixture. Pass through fine sieve. Return to heat. Add cream, port and armagnac. Simmer for 5 minutes, stirring from time to time. Add the cold butter in pieces. Season. Add lemon juice.

CRAB AND GINGER FILLING
See Ménage à Trois fillings.

CRAB MOUSSE, COLD
1 shallot, finely chopped/$\frac{1}{4}$ stick (2 Tbsp) unsalted butter, clarified/1 tsp Dijon mustard/1 Tbsp armagnac/1 tsp tomato purée/brown meat from 3lb cooked crab/$1\frac{1}{2}$c fish stock (*page 142*)/2 sheets gelatin softened in cold water/salt and white pepper/$1\frac{1}{4}$c whipping cream/3 egg whites
Sweat shallot in butter. Add mustard, armagnac and tomato purée. Add crab, then fish stock. Bring to boil. Reduce until most liquid has evaporated. Add gelatin. Liquidize and pass through a fine sieve. Leave to cool. Season. Whip cream to soft peaks. Fold in. Beat egg whites to soft peaks. Fold in carefully. Leave to set in refrigerator. (Makes approx. 1c.)

CRANBERRY SAUCE See under Cranberries in Notes on Ingredients, *page 151*.

CREAMED EGG MOUSSE
4 eggs/4 Tbsp heavy cream/1 shallot, finely chopped/$\frac{1}{4}$ stick (2 Tbsp) unsalted butter, clarified/1 tsp horseradish cream (*page 143*)/ 1 tsp chopped chives/salt and black pepper
Break eggs neatly, reserving shells for serving. Beat with fork. Add cream. Pass through fine sieve to break down egg white. Sweat shallot in butter until soft but not brown. Add egg mixture, horseradish cream and chives. Cook over medium heat in non-stick or Teflon pan, whisking. Season. Remove when it starts to set, cool and refrigerate. (Makes approx. $\frac{1}{2}$c).

CUCUMBER AND MINT SAUCE
Use champagne and cucumber sauce recipe (*page 140*). Replace rosemary

with chopped mint stalks. Replace champagne with dry white wine. Add julienned mint leaves with the cream.

DARK TRUFFLE SAUCE See Truffle sauce, dark.

DEMI-GLAZE See note on stocks on *page 140*.

DILL CREAM See Dill sauce.

DILL MAYONNAISE

I egg/juice of 2 lemons (reserve peel for decoration)/I tsp sugar/I tsp Dijon mustard/2 Tbsp chopped dill weed/salt and pepper/approx. $\frac{1}{2}$c 2 Tbsp olive oil

Blend all ingredients except oil in blender. Keep machine running. Add oil gradually until desired consistency is reached. The more oil, the thicker the mayonnaise. (Makes approx. $\frac{1}{2}$c 2 Tbsp.)

DILL SAUCE OR CREAM

3 Tbsp chopped dill stalks/I shallot, chopped/$\frac{1}{2}$ clove garlic, chopped/I glass dry white wine/I$\frac{1}{4}$c stock/I$\frac{1}{4}$c heavy cream/2 Tbsp chopped dill leaves/salt and white pepper/$\frac{1}{4}$ stick (2 Tbsp) cold unsalted butter/squeeze of lemon juice

Add first 4 ingredients to stock. Bring to a boil. Reduce by $\frac{3}{4}$. Strain through fine sieve. Add cream and chopped dill leaves. Simmer for 5 minutes. Add cold butter in pieces. Season. Add lemon juice. You can also add I tsp Pernod or Ricard. Omit the butter if making a cold dill cream.

DRY VERMOUTH AND CHERVIL SAUCE Use champagne sauce recipe (*page 140*). Replace champagne with $\frac{1}{2}$ cup dry white vermouth. Add at start: sprig of rosemary/I clove garlic, chopped. Add at end: I tsp each chopped chervil and parsley.

DUCK STOCK Use chicken stock recipe (*page 141*) with duck carcasses in place of chicken.

DUXELLE OF WILD MUSHROOMS, COLD

2 shallots, finely chopped/I clove garlic, finely chopped/I Tbsp peanut oil/$\frac{1}{4}$ stick (2 Tbsp) unsalted butter, clarified/2$\frac{1}{2}$c finely diced wild mushrooms or trimmings/salt and black pepper

Sweat shallot and garlic in oil and butter until soft. Add mushrooms. Raise heat. Cook, stirring occasionally, until mushroom juice has evaporated. Season. Refrigerate until needed. (Makes approx. $\frac{1}{2}$c.)

EGG MOUSSE, CREAMED See Creamed egg mousse.

EGGPLANT MOUSSE, HOT

I shallot, finely chopped/I clove garlic, finely chopped/$\frac{1}{4}$ stick (2 Tbsp) unsalted butter, clarified/3 medium eggplants, peeled and diced/sprig of thyme/2c vegetable stock (*page 148*)/$\frac{1}{4}$c heavy cream/2 whole eggs/salt and black pepper

Sweat shallot and garlic in butter. Add eggplants and thyme. Add stock. Bring to a boil. Simmer until eggplants soften. Remove them. Strain stock and return to heat. Reduce to 2 Tbsp. Return eggplants. Cool a little. Mix cream with eggs and add. Liquidize. Pass through fine sieve. Season. Refrigerate until needed. Cook as in recipe or in a bain-marie in a medium oven. (Makes approx. 1c.)

FIG COULIS

8 dried figs/3 Tbsp port/3 Tbsp brandy/$\frac{1}{2}$c water/$\frac{3}{4}$ stick (6 Tbsp) unsalted butter, clarified/salt and black pepper

Discard fig stalks. Chop figs. Soak in port and brandy for at least 45 minutes. Transfer to saucepan. Add water and $\frac{1}{3}$ butter. Cover. Simmer for 30 minutes or until most liquid has been absorbed. Purée with remaining butter. Pass through sieve. Season. Refrigerate until needed. (Makes approx. 6 Tbsp.)

FISH STOCK

3lb bones and heads from white fish, skin and gills removed/2c dry white wine/I stick celery/white of 2 leeks/2 Tbsp mushroom trimmings/I onion, peeled and stuck with 2 cloves/I bouquet garni/a few parsley stalks/juice of I lemon/I tsp crushed white peppercorns

Soak bones and heads in iced salted water for 30 minutes. Break up bones. Put in saucepan with other ingredients. Cover with water. Bring to a boil. Simmer for 20 minutes (no longer), skimming regularly. Strain through fine sieve lined with paper towel or wet cheesecloth. Return to heat and boil until reduced to 2$\frac{1}{2}$c.

GAME MOUSSE, HOT

3 Tbsp meat glaze (*page 140*)/I Tbsp red currant jelly/I shallot, finely chopped/I clove garlic, finely chopped/sprig of thyme/Ic sliced mushrooms/$\frac{1}{4}$ stick (2 Tbsp) unsalted butter, clarified/$\frac{1}{2}$lb meat from breasts of old birds (pheasant, partridge etc.)/I Tbsp brandy/I Tbsp port/pinch of grated nutmeg/I whole egg + 2 whites/black pepper/2$\frac{1}{2}$c heavy cream/I$\frac{1}{2}$ tsp salt

Heat meat glaze and red currant jelly until melted. Set aside. Sweat shallot, garlic, thyme and mushrooms in butter until soft but not brown. Leave to cool. Trim skin and gristle from meat. Put in food processor with shallot mixture, glaze mixture, brandy, port and nutmeg. Process until smooth. Add egg and egg whites. Pass through fine sieve into bowl set over ice. Add pepper. Add cream and salt slowly, working in with wooden spoon. Refrigerate until needed. Cook as in recipe or in a bain-marie in a medium oven. (Makes approx. $1\frac{1}{2}$c.)

GAME STOCK

4lb game carcasses, venison bones etc./1 veal foreshank/2 whole onions, each stuck with 2 cloves/1 carrot, thinly sliced/2 cloves garlic, crushed/1 stick celery, sliced/2 leeks, sliced/1 bottle red wine/1 bouquet garni/1 Tbsp roasted and crushed juniper berries/1 blade mace/1 tsp crushed white peppercorns/5c golden veal stock (*page 148*).

Roast bones and vegetables as in golden veal stock recipe, deglazing with some of the wine. Put all ingredients in large pot with $2\frac{1}{2}$qt water. Bring to a boil. Simmer for 4 hours, skimming regularly and adding more water if needed. Strain through fine sieve lined with paper towels or wet cheesecloth. Leave to settle. Remove fat from top. Return to heat. Reduce to 3c.

GARLIC CREAM

3 bulbs garlic, split into cloves, each one peeled and halved/1 stick ($\frac{1}{2}$c) unsalted butter, clarified/1 large onion, sliced/1 bay leaf/salt and white pepper/heavy cream as required

Boil garlic in 3 changes of boiling water for 5 minutes each time. Drain. Put butter in saucepan. Add onion, bay leaf and garlic. Cook gently for 35 minutes, stirring occasionally. Season. Discard bay leaf. Liquidize. Pass through fine sieve. Dilute with cream to required consistency. Refrigerate until needed.

GIN AND JUNIPER SAUCE

Add to marinade once meat has been removed (*page 144*), $1\frac{1}{2}$c golden veal stock (*page 148*) and 2 Tbsp crushed and roasted juniper berries. Boil until reduced by half. Stir in $\frac{1}{2}$ stick ($\frac{1}{4}$c) cold unsalted butter, a piece at a time. Just before serving add 2 Tbsp gin.

GLAZE, FULL See note on stocks on *page 140*.

GOLDEN VEAL STOCK See Veal stock, golden.

HARE AND PRUNE FILLING See Ménage à Trois fillings.

HAZELNUT OIL DRESSING See Walnut oil dressing.

HOLLANDAISE SAUCE

5 Tbsp white wine vinegar/4 Tbsp water/$\frac{1}{2}$tsp crushed white peppercorns/1 bay leaf/4 egg yolks/2 sticks (1c) cold unsalted butter/salt

Boil vinegar, water, peppercorns and bay leaf until reduced to 2 Tbsp. Strain into double boiler. When slightly cooled, stir in egg yolks. Keep double boiler over low heat. Add butter in small cubes, one at a time, stirring constantly to blend each in completely before adding the next. Sauce will gradually thicken. Avoid overheating, which will curdle it. Season. Cover sauce with wax paper and keep in a warm place until needed. It will only keep for a short time, and cannot be reheated. The sooner it is served, the better it tastes. (Makes approx. 1c.)

HORSERADISH AND ONION SAUCE

$\frac{3}{4}$lb white onions, finely sliced/1 clove garlic, chopped/$\frac{1}{4}$ stick (2 Tbsp) unsalted butter, clarified/$1\frac{1}{4}$c stock/1 bay leaf/2 sage leaves/$1\frac{1}{4}$c heavy cream/1 Tbsp horseradish cream (*below*)/$\frac{1}{4}$ stick (2 Tbsp) cold unsalted butter/salt and white pepper/dash of Worcester sauce

Sweat onions and garlic in clarified butter until soft, not brown. Add stock, bay leaf and sage. Bring to a boil. Reduce by half. Discard bay leaf. Liquidize stock, cream and horseradish. Return to heat. Skim. Add cold butter in small pieces. Season with salt and pepper. Add Worcester sauce.

HORSERADISH CREAM

$\frac{1}{2}$c whipping cream/2 Tbsp grated horseradish/3 Tbsp lemon juice/$\frac{3}{4}$tsp salt/$\frac{1}{8}$tsp paprika/pinch of cayenne

Beat cream until stiff. Fold in other ingredients a little at a time. Refrigerate until needed. Use within 2 days.

JELLIED STOCK See stocks, *page 140*, and veal, beef, chicken or game jelly.

LEEK AND ROQUEFORT MOUSSE, COLD

1lb leeks, roughly chopped/$1\frac{1}{4}$c vegetable stock (*page 148*)/2 shallots, finely chopped/1 clove garlic, finely chopped/2 leaves sage/$\frac{1}{4}$ stick (2 Tbsp) unsalted butter, clarified/4 sheets gelatin softened in cold water/$\frac{1}{2}$lb Roquefort/salt and black pepper/$1\frac{1}{2}$c whipping cream/4 egg whites

Boil leeks in vegetable stock until tender. Meanwhile sweat shallot, garlic and sage in butter until soft. Strain leeks, reserving stock. Return stock to heat. Reduce to $\frac{3}{4}$c. Add gelatin. Let cool a little. Add Rouqefort and leeks to shallots. Stir until cheese has melted. Add stock. Liquidize. Pass through medium sieve. Season. Leave to cool. Whip cream to soft peaks. Fold into mixture. Whip egg whites to soft peaks. Stir in 1 Tbsp: fold in the rest. Leave to set in refrigerator. (Makes approx. $1\frac{1}{2}$c.)

LOBSTER AND MINTED PEA FILLING See Ménage à Trois fillings.

LOBSTER AND SPINACH MOUSSE, HOT

$\frac{3}{4}$lb uncooked lobster meat, including coral/ 6oz spinach, cooked, drained and finely chopped/2 whole eggs + 2 whites/2c heavy cream/1$\frac{1}{2}$tsp salt

Blend lobster meat and spinach in food processor until smooth. Blend in eggs and whites. Pass through fine sieve into bowl set over ice. Work in cream and salt gradually with wooden spoon. Refrigerate until needed. Cook as in recipe or in a bain-marie in a medium oven. (Makes approx. 1$\frac{3}{4}$c.)

MANGO COULIS

2 ripe mangoes, peeled, pitted and chopped/ $\frac{1}{2}$ bottle champagne or sparkling wine/2 Tbsp honey/juice of $\frac{1}{2}$ lemon

Liquidize all ingredients. Pass through fine sieve. Instead of champagne, a mixture of vegetable stock (*page 148*) and dry white wine can be used. Refrigerate until needed. (Makes approx. 2$\frac{1}{2}$c.)

MARINADE, COOKED, FOR GAME, FISH OR POULTRY

1 carrot, thinly sliced/1 stick celery, chopped/1 onion, thinly sliced/2 cloves garlic, chopped/3 Tbsp olive oil/2$\frac{1}{2}$c red or white wine/2 Tbsp red or white wine vinegar/1 Tbsp crushed coriander seeds/1 Tbsp roasted and crushed juniper berries/2c water

Use red wine and red wine vinegar for dark meats. Sweat vegetables in oil for 10 minutes. Add other ingredients. Bring to a boil. Simmer for 35 minutes. Strain. This marinade can also be used uncooked, in which case do not strain and marinate the meat for about 2 hours longer.

MEAT GLAZE See note on stocks on *page 140*.

MEAT STOCK See chicken stock

recipe (*page 141*) with beef bones instead of chicken carcass.

MÉNAGE À TROIS FILLINGS

For assembly, see *page 138*.

CRAB AND GINGER (8 parcels)

1 shallot, finely chopped/1 clove garlic, finely chopped/2 tsp finely chopped ginger/$\frac{1}{4}$ stick (2 Tbsp) unsalted butter, clarified/ white meat from 2lb cooked crab/ $\frac{1}{4}$ cucumber, peeled, seeded and finely diced/ $\frac{1}{4}$c saffron and ginger sauce (*page 146*)/salt and black pepper

Sweat shallot, garlic and ginger slowly in butter until soft but not brown. Add crab, cucumber and sauce. Bring to a boil. Season. Cool before use.

HARE AND PRUNE (4 parcels)

4 prunes, soaked in brandy and tea/ $\frac{1}{2}$ shallot, chopped/1 small clove garlic, chopped/$\frac{1}{8}$ stick (1 Tbsp) unsalted butter, clarified/$\frac{1}{4}$lb marinated hare meat, diced/2 Tbsp sour cream/salt and cayenne pepper

Cook prunes in soaking liquid for 20 minutes. Let cool. Drain, halve and pit them. Keep 4 halves, dice rest. Sweat shallot and garlic in butter until soft but not brown. Add drained meat and diced prunes. Raise heat. Cook for 2 minutes. Add sour cream. Cook for 30 seconds, stirring. Season. Cool before use. Put a prune half on pastry and top with mixture.

LOBSTER AND MINTED PEA (4 parcels)

$\frac{1}{4}$c pea and mint purée (*opposite*)/$\frac{1}{4}$lb cooked lobster meat/2 Tbsp cold champagne sauce (*page 140*)

Place ingredients on pastry in above order.

PIGEON, RED CABBAGE AND APPLE (8 parcels)

2oz bacon/1 Tbsp goose fat/2$\frac{1}{2}$c finely chopped red cabbage without stalk/2 apples, peeled, cored and finely diced/2 Tbsp raisins, soaked in brandy/1 Tbsp red currant jelly/1 Tbsp port/3 Tbsp game stock (*page 143*)/salt and black pepper/pinch of grated nutmeg/1 shallot, finely chopped/2 pigeon breasts, skinned, boned and diced/3 Tbsp game glaze (see note on stocks on *page 140*)

Brown bacon in half goose fat. Add cabbage, apple, raisins and red currant jelly. Stir. Add port and stock. Cover. Cook slowly for 2 hours. Season. Add nutmeg. Leave to cool. Sweat shallot in rest of goose fat until soft. Add pigeon. Raise heat and sauté for 2 minutes. Add meat glaze. Cook for 30 seconds. Season. Put spoonful of cabbage mixture on pastry. Top with spoonful of pigeon.

TURBOT AND LEEK (4 parcels)

4 × 1 inch cubes turbot/salt and white pepper/squeeze of lemon juice/4 Tbsp leek julienne softened in butter.

Season fish: sprinkle with lemon juice. Steam for 1 minute. Let cool. Put a spoonful of leek mixture on pastry. Top with turbot.

VENISON AND CRANBERRY (4 parcels)

$\frac{1}{2}$ shallot, finely chopped/$\frac{1}{2}$ tsp finely chopped garlic/$\frac{1}{8}$ stick (1 Tbsp) unsalted butter, clarified/$\frac{1}{4}$lb venison, finely diced/2 Tbsp cranberry sauce (page 151)/1 Tbsp game glaze (see note on stocks page 140)/ 1 Tbsp brandy/salt and black pepper

Sweat shallot and garlic in butter until soft. Add venison. Raise heat and cook for 2 minutes. Add cranberry sauce, game glaze and brandy. Season. Let cool before use.

MINTED ORANGE SAUCE

juice of 3 oranges/juice of $\frac{1}{2}$ lemon/1 shallot, chopped/1 bay leaf/2 Tbsp chopped mint stalks/$1\frac{1}{4}$c stock/$1\frac{1}{4}$c cream/$\frac{1}{4}$ stick (2 Tbsp) cold unsalted butter/1 Tbsp mint leaves, julienned/salt and white pepper/1 Tbsp mint vinegar

Add first 5 ingredients to stock. Bring to a boil. Reduce by two-thirds. Strain. Add cream. Simmer for 5 minutes. Add butter in small pieces. Add mint. Season, Add vinegar.

MOREL MOUSSE OR SAUCE

Use wild mushroom mousse or sauce recipe (page 149). Omit garlic in the mushroom sauce recipe. Use morels whenever other mushrooms are mentioned. Reserve a few rings of cooked morel to garnish.

MUSHROOM MOUSSE OR SAUCE See Wild mushroom mousse or sauce.

NETTLE AND SORREL SAUCE

2 Tbsp chopped shallot/1 clove garlic, chopped/1 sage leaf/$\frac{1}{4}$ stick (2 Tbsp) unsalted butter, clarified/8 young sorrel leaves/16 young nettle leaves/2c stock (page 140)/1 bay leaf/$\frac{1}{2}$c dry white wine/$1\frac{1}{4}$c heavy cream/$\frac{1}{4}$ stick (2 Tbsp) cold unsalted butter/ salt and black pepper

Sweat shallot, garlic and sage in clarified butter until soft. Add sorrel and nettles. Allow their juices to sweat out. Add stock, bay leaf and wine. Bring to a boil. Reduce by half. Liquidize. Pass through fine sieve. Add cream. Simmer

for 5 minutes. Add cold butter in small pieces. Season.

OYSTER AND CHAMPAGNE SAUCE

Use champagne sauce recipe (page 140), adding strained juice from 12 oysters at the start. Finish as usual, adding diced oysters if you like.

PEA AND MINT PURÉE

1 clove garlic, finely chopped/3 scallions, finely sliced/$\frac{1}{4}$ stick (2 Tbsp) unsalted butter, clarified/$\frac{1}{2}$lb shelled peas/1 head lettuce, shredded/1 tsp sugar/$1\frac{1}{2}$c vegetable stock/2 Tbsp finely chopped mint leaves/2 Tbsp heavy cream/salt and black pepper

Sweat garlic and scallions in butter until soft. Add peas, lettuce, sugar and stock. Cook until peas are tender. Strain and return liquid to pan. Bring to a boil. Add mint. Reduce to 2 Tbsp. Add cream and peas. Liquidize. Season. (Makes approx. $\frac{3}{4}$c.)

PESTO See Basil sauce under Basil in Notes in Ingredients, page 150.

PIGEON, RED CABBAGE AND APPLE FILLING See Ménage à Trois fillings.

PORT AND CRANBERRY SAUCE

Use port and orange sauce recipe (below), but with juice of only 1 orange. Replace red currant jelly with cranberry sauce.

PORT AND ORANGE SAUCE

$\frac{1}{2}$c 2 Tbsp golden veal stock (page 148)/$\frac{1}{2}$c 2 Tbsp dry red wine/juice of 3 oranges/juice of $\frac{1}{2}$ lemon/2 Tbsp red currant jelly/1 shallot, chopped/1 clove garlic, chopped/$\frac{1}{2}$ tsp chopped ginger/sprig of thyme/1 bay leaf/$\frac{1}{4}$c ruby port/$\frac{2}{3}$ stick (5 Tbsp) cold unsalted butter/1 Tbsp raspberry vinegar

Put first 10 ingredients in a pan. Bring to a boil. Reduce by three-quarters, skimming regularly. Strain. Add port. Simmer 5 minutes. Add butter in small pieces. Season. Add vinegar.

PUMPKIN SAUCE

$1\frac{1}{3}$c peeled and finely diced pumpkin/1 shallot, chopped/1 clove garlic, chopped/1 sage leaf/pinch of grated nutmeg/1 tomato purée/1 tsp sugar/$2\frac{1}{2}$c stock/$\frac{2}{3}$c grated Emmenthal/$1\frac{1}{4}$c heavy cream/$\frac{1}{4}$ stick (2 Tbsp) cold unsalted butter/salt and white pepper/squeeze of lemon juice

Add first 7 ingredients to stock. Bring to a boil. Cook until pumpkin is soft. Add Emmanthal. Simmer until melted. Discard sage. Liquidize. Pass through fine sieve. Add cream. Simmer for 5 minutes, adding extra stock if too thick.

Add butter in small pieces. Season. Add lemon juice. Made slightly thinner, this is an excellent soup.

RAVIOLI FILLING

3oz duck foie gras/salt and black pepper/1 small truffle, cooked, peeled and finely chopped/2 Tbsp wild mushroom duxelle (*page 142*)/2 Tbsp heavy cream

Sauté foie gras in hot pan, without added fat, for 20 seconds each side. Let cool. Season. Dice finely. Mix with truffle, duxelle and cream. Refrigerate until needed.

RED BURGUNDY SAUCE

2 shallots, chopped/1 clove garlic, chopped/$\frac{1}{4}$ stick (2 Tbsp) unsalted butter, clarified/2 Tbsp flour/2c stock/$1\frac{1}{4}$c red burgundy/1 bay leaf/sprig of thyme/1 tsp sugar/3 Tbsp mushroom trimmings/$\frac{1}{4}$ stick (2 Tbsp) cold unsalted butter/salt and black pepper

Sweat shallot and garlic in clarified butter until soft and golden. Sprinkle with flour. Mix well. Add stock, wine, bay leaf, thyme, sugar and mushroom trimmings. Bring to a boil. Reduce by two-thirds. Strain. Add cold butter in small pieces. Season. You can also add at end poached, diced bone marrow.

ROQUEFORT CREAM

$\frac{1}{2}$c still hard cider/white of 2 medium leeks/1 clove garlic, chopped/2 sage leaves/2c stock/$\frac{1}{4}$lb Roquefort/$1\frac{1}{4}$c heavy cream/salt and white pepper/squeeze of lemon juice

Add first 4 ingredients to stock. Bring to a boil. Reduce by half. Add Roquefort. Simmer gently until melted. Add cream. Liquidize. Strain through fine sieve. Season. Add lemon juice. Thin if necessary with extra stock.

ROSEMARY SAUCE Use

champagne sauce recipe (*page 140*). Replace champagne with dry white vermouth. Replace thyme with 6 sprigs of rosemary.

SAFFRON AND GINGER SAUCE

1 shallot, chopped/1 clove garlic, chopped/sprig of thyme/2 tsp chopped fresh ginger/$\frac{1}{2}$c dry white wine/pinch of grated nutmeg/$1\frac{1}{4}$c stock/$1\frac{1}{4}$c heavy cream/1 tsp more finely chopped fresh ginger/$\frac{1}{2}$ tsp saffron soaked in 1 Tbsp warm stock/$\frac{1}{4}$ stick (2 Tbsp) cold unsalted butter/salt and white pepper/squeeze of lemon juice

Add first 6 ingredients to stock. Bring to a boil. Reduce by two-thirds. Strain through fine sieve. Add cream, ginger and saffron. Simmer for 5 minutes. Add butter in small pieces. Whisk. Season. Add lemon juice.

SCALLOP MOUSSE, COLD

$\frac{1}{2}$lb scallops without shells/$\frac{1}{4}$c dry white vermouth/$\frac{1}{2}$ shallot, chopped/$\frac{1}{4}$ stick (2 Tbsp) unsalted butter, clarified/$1\frac{1}{2}$c fish stock (*page 142*)/sprig of thyme/2 sheets gelatin, softened in cold water/salt and white pepper/$1\frac{1}{4}$c whipping cream/3 egg whites

Slice scallops thinly. Cook in vermouth for 20 seconds. Drain. Sweat shallot in butter until soft but not brown. Add the vermouth, fish stock and thyme. Reduce to $\frac{1}{2}$c, Remove thyme. Add gelatin and scallops. Liquidize. Pass through fine sieve. Season. Whip cream to soft peaks. Fold into mixture. Whip egg whites to soft peaks. Fold in carefully. Leave to set in refrigerator. (Makes approx. 1c.)

SCALLOP MOUSSE, HOT

$\frac{1}{2}$lb scallops without shells/2 Tbsp dry white vermouth/1 whole egg + 1 white/$1\frac{1}{2}$c heavy cream/1 tsp salt/white pepper

Put scallops and vermouth in food processor. Blend. Add egg and white. Blend for 1 minute. Pass through fine sieve into bowl over ice. Work cream and salt gradually into mixture with wooden spoon. Add pepper. Refrigerate until needed. Cook as in recipe or in a bain-marie in a medium oven. (Makes approx. 1c.)

SESAME OIL DRESSING

3 scallions, chopped/1 Tbsp chopped ginger/4 cloves garlic, chopped/3 Tbsp sesame oil/1 Tbsp honey/1 Tbsp soy sauce/$\frac{1}{2}$ tsp five spice powder/1 Tbsp chopped cilantro/$1\frac{1}{2}$c chicken stock (*page 141*)/salt and black pepper

Sweat scallions, ginger and garlic in sesame oil until soft but not brown. Add honey, soy sauce, five spice powder, cilantro and chicken stock. Simmer for 15 minutes. Season. Leave to cool. Strain.

SMOKED COD'S ROE SAUCE, COLD

$\frac{1}{2}$lb smoked cod's roe/1 shallot, finely chopped/2 cloves garlic, finely chopped/1 Tbsp olive oil/juice of 1 lemon/1 tsp tomato purée/1 Tbsp chopped chives/dash of Worcester sauce/dash of Tabasco sauce/black pepper/$1\frac{1}{2}$c whipping cream

Cut roe in half. Scrape out inside with small spoon. Discard skin. Sweat shallot and garlic in oil. Leave to cool. Blend roe, shallot, garlic, lemon juice and tomato purée in food processor until smooth. Add chives. Worcester sauce, Tabasco sauce and pepper. Transfer to a bowl. Stir in cream. If a stiff texture is preferred, first whip cream. Leave in the refrigerator until needed. (Makes approx. $2\frac{1}{2}$c.)

SMOKED SALMON MOUSSE, COLD

$\frac{1}{2}$ shallot, finely chopped/$\frac{1}{2}$ clove garlic, finely chopped/$\frac{1}{8}$ stick (1 Tbsp) unsalted butter, clarified/1 tsp tomato purée/$1\frac{1}{2}$c fish stock (page 142)/2 sheets gelatin, softened in cold water/6oz smoked salmon pieces/pinch of cayenne pepper/juice of $\frac{1}{2}$ lemon/$1\frac{1}{2}$c whipping cream/3 egg whites

Sweat shallot and garlic in butter. Add tomato purée and fish stock. Boil until reduced to 2 Tbsp. Add gelatin and smoked salmon. Liquidize. Pass through fine sieve. Add cayenne and lemon juice. Whip cream to soft peaks. Fold into salmon purée. Whip whites to soft peaks. Fold in carefully. Leave to set in refrigerator. (Makes approx. 1c.)

SOUR CREAM DRESSING

$1\frac{1}{2}$c sour cream/2 Tbsp finely chopped scallions/1 tsp Worcester sauce/2 small gherkins, finely chopped/juice of $\frac{1}{2}$ lemon/ salt and cayenne pepper

Mix all ingredients, seasoning to taste.

SPINACH AND DILL MOUSSE,
HOT Use spinach mousse recipe (below). Add with the shallot and garlic a handful of chopped dill weed.

SPINACH CREAM See Spinach sauce.

SPINACH MOUSSE, HOT

$1\frac{1}{2}$lb spinach/$\frac{3}{4}$c vegetable stock (page 148)/2 shallots, chopped/1 clove garlic, chopped/$\frac{1}{2}$ stick ($\frac{1}{4}$c) unsalted butter, clarified/salt and black pepper/1 whole egg + 2 yolks/4 Tbsp heavy cream/1 tsp chlorophyll coloring (page 141)/more butter for molds

Cook spinach quickly in vegetable stock until tender. Drain, reserving stock. When cool, squeeze out liquid. Boil liquid and reserved stock until reduced to 2 Tbsp. Sweat shallot and garlic in butter until soft but not brown. Add spinach and stock. Season. Liquidize. Add egg, yolks, cream and chlorophyll coloring. Pass through fine sieve. Cook as in recipe or as for celery root mousse (page 140). (Makes approx. $\frac{3}{4}$c.)

SPINACH SAUCE OR CREAM
Use nettle and sorrel sauce recipe (page 145). Replace sorrel and nettle with equal amount of spinach. After adding cream, add $\frac{1}{2}$ tsp chlorophyll coloring (page 141). Omit addition of cold butter for cold spinach cream.

STOCKS See note on stocks (page 140), Chicken stock, Fish stock, Game stock, Veal stock, golden, and Vegetable stock.

TOMATO AND BASIL SAUCE

2 tsp chopped shallot/$\frac{1}{2}$c dry white wine/4 tomatoes, peeled, seeded and chopped/2 Tbsp basil sauce (pesto, page 150)/1 tsp tomato purée/$1\frac{1}{4}$c stock/$1\frac{1}{4}$c heavy cream/ $\frac{1}{4}$ stick (2 Tbsp) cold unsalted butter/salt and white pepper/1 Tbsp julienned basil leaves/1 Tbsp champagne vinegar

Add first 5 ingredients to stock. Bring to a boil. Reduce by half. Liquidize. Pass through fine sieve. Add cream. Simmer for 5 minutes. Add butter in small pieces. Season. Add basil and vinegar.

TOMATO AND GARLIC SAUCE
Use tomato and basil sauce recipe (above). Omit basil sauce and basil. Add 3 Tbsp garlic cream (page 143) to the cream.

TOMATO AND ROSEMARY
SAUCE Use tomato and basil sauce recipe (above). Omit basil sauce and basil. Add 4 sprigs of rosemary at start; remove before liquidizing.

TOMATO CONCASSÉ (PULP).
COOKED

2 shallots, finely chopped/2 cloves garlic, finely chopped/2 sprigs of thyme/$\frac{1}{4}$ stick (2 Tbsp) unsalted butter, clarified/1lb tomatoes, peeled, seeded and diced/1 tsp sugar/salt and white pepper

Sweat shallot, garlic and thyme in butter until soft but not brown. Add tomatoes and sugar. Cook over medium heat for 15 minutes. Remove thyme. Season. (Makes approx. $\frac{3}{4}$c.)

TOMATO COULIS, UNCOOKED
This beautiful light pink dressing is quite different from a cooked tomato sauce.

2 shallots, finely chopped/1 clove garlic, finely chopped/$1\frac{1}{2}$c olive oil/1lb tomatoes, peeled, seeded and chopped/1 tsp Dijon mustard/1 whole egg/3 Tbsp cider and honey vinegar/salt and white pepper/1 tsp chopped herbs as liked

Sweat shallot and garlic in 1 Tbsp oil until soft but not brown. Leave to cool. Put in food processor with tomatoes, mustard, egg and vinegar. Blend until smooth. With blender running, add oil slowly to form emulsion. Pass through fine sieve. Season and add herbs. (Makes approx. $1\frac{1}{4}$c.)

TRUFFLE SAUCE, DARK

2c golden veal stock (page 148)/3 Tbsp truffle juice/1 tsp mushroom ketchup/3

Tbsp mushroom trimmings (wild if possible)/
1 shallot, chopped/pinch of grated nutmeg/
2 extra Tbsp truffle juice/1 Tbsp port/2 tsp
armagnac/$\frac{2}{3}$ stick (5 Tbsp) cold unsalted
butter/1 tsp truffle or truffle peeling, diced/
salt and black pepper
Boil together first 6 ingredients. Reduce
by half. Strain. Add extra truffle juice,
port and armagnac. Simmer for 3
minutes. Skim. Add butter in small
pieces. Season. Add diced truffle.

TRUFFLE SAUCE, WHITE
1 shallot, chopped/2 tsp mushroom
trimmings (wild if possible)/1 bay leaf/3 Tbsp
truffle juice/1 tsp mushroom ketchup/1$\frac{1}{4}$c
vegetable stock/1$\frac{1}{4}$c heavy cream/3 more
Tbsp truffle juice/2 tsp armagnac/4 tsp port/
$\frac{1}{4}$ stick (2 Tbsp) cold unsalted butter/salt and
white pepper/1 Tbsp champagne vinegar
Add first 5 ingredients to stock. Bring to
a boil. Reduce by two-thirds. Strain.
Add cream, extra truffle juice,
armagnac and port. Simmer for 5
minutes. Add butter in small pieces.
Season. Add vinegar. You can also add
at the end 1 Tbsp white truffle peelings,
chopped.

TURBOT AND LEEK FILLING See
Ménage à Trois fillings.

VEAL, BEEF, CHICKEN OR
GAME JELLY
3lb veal or beef bones or chicken or game
carcasses, chopped/2 calf's feet, chopped/
1 onion, chopped/1 bouquet garni/$\frac{1}{2}$lb veal
foreshank or chicken or game scraps, finely
chopped/1 more onion, finely chopped/1
leek, finely chopped/1 carrot, sliced/2 egg
whites
Put bones or carcasses with feet, 1
onion and bouquet garni in large pot.
Cover with water. Bring to a boil.
Simmer for as long as possible (at least
6 hours), keeping covered with water
and skimming regularly. Strain
through fine sieve lined with wet paper
towel or cheesecloth. Mix chopped
meat and vegetables with egg whites.
Add to stock. Bring to a boil very
slowly, stirring constantly. Once
simmering, leave for 30 minutes
without stirring. Strain through
cheesecloth-lined sieve. Liquid will be
clear. Leave to cool. (Makes approx.
1$\frac{1}{4}$c.)

VEAL STOCK, GOLDEN
3lb veal marrow bones, broken/2 carrots,
sliced/2 onions, sliced/2$\frac{1}{2}$c mushroom
trimmings/1 small stick celery, sliced/
$\frac{1}{2}$ bottle dry white wine/1 bouquet garni/

1 clove garlic, crushed/3 tomatoes, peeled and
seeded/1 Tbsp tomato purée
Brown bones in hot oven, turning
regularly. After 20 minutes add carrots,
onions, mushroom trimmings and
celery. Cook for 10 minutes more.
Transfer all to large saucepan. Deglaze
roasting tray with white wine. Pour
into saucepan. Add bouquet garni and
garlic. Add 2$\frac{1}{2}$qt water. Bring to a boil.
Simmer, skimming regularly, for 4
hours, adding tomatoes and purée after
2 hours. There should be about 3$\frac{3}{4}$c
liquid left. Pass through fine sieve lined
with paper towel or wet cheesecloth.
Cool and carefully remove fat. White
veal stock is made in exactly the same
way, but without browning the bones
at the beginning.

VEGETABLE STOCK
2c dry white wine/4 tomatoes, peeled and
seeded/2 leeks, washed and sliced/1 carrot,
peeled and sliced/1 stick celery, sliced/1
onion, peeled and stuck with 2 cloves/4
cloves garlic, sliced/1 bouquet garni/1 tsp
white peppercorns, crushed/1 Tbsp
mushrooms peelings
Place all ingredients in a large
saucepan. Cover with water and bring
to a boil. Simmer for 2$\frac{1}{2}$ hours,
skimming regularly. Pass through a
fine sieve line with paper towel or wet
cheesecloth. (Makes approx. 1$\frac{1}{4}$c.)

VENISON AND CRANBERRY
FILLING See Ménage à Trois fillings.

WALNUT OIL DRESSING
$\frac{1}{2}$c walnut oil/$\frac{1}{2}$c peanut oil/$\frac{1}{2}$ tsp Dijon
mustard/1 shallot, finely chopped/1 clove
garlic, finely chopped/juice of 1 lemon/3
Tbsp champagne vinegar/1 bay leaf/sprig of
tarragon/salt and black pepper/$\frac{1}{2}$ tsp sugar
Blend all ingredients with hand whisk.
Leave to settle for up to 24 hours. Pass
through fine sieve. Whisk before using.
A hazelnut oil dressing can be made in
the same way, using hazelnut oil
instead of walnut.

WATERCRESS CREAM
Use broccoli sauce recipe (page 140).
Omit rosemary. Replace broccoli with
watercress, using stalks as with
broccoli. Blanch leaves for 30 seconds
before adding with cream. Continue as
in recipe, omitting cold butter at the
end.

WHITE TRUFFLE SAUCE See
Truffle sauce, white.

WILD MUSHROOM DUXELLE See
Duxelle of wild mushrooms.

WILD MUSHROOM MOUSSE.HOT

$\frac{1}{4}$c duxelle of wild mushrooms (*page 142*)/$\frac{3}{4}$c vegetable stock (*opposite*)/salt and black pepper/2 whole eggs + 2 whites/2 Tbsp heavy cream

Simmer duxelle in stock until most liquid is reduced. Liquidize. Season. Mix eggs and whites with cream and add to mixture. Refrigerate until needed. Cook as in recipe or in a bain-marie in a medium oven. (Makes approx. 6 Tbsp.)

WILD MUSHROOM SAUCE

4 Tbsp wild mushroom trimmings/1 shallot, chopped/1 clove garlic, chopped/$\frac{1}{2}$c dry white wine/pinch of grated nutmeg/$1\frac{1}{2}$c vegetable stock (*opposite*)/1 more shallot, chopped/1 more clove garlic, chopped/$\frac{1}{4}$ stick (2 Tbsp) unsalted butter, clarified/2c sliced wild mushrooms/$1\frac{1}{4}$c heavy cream/3 Tbsp truffle juice/$\frac{1}{4}$ stick (2 Tbsp) cold unsalted butter/salt and black pepper

Add first 5 ingredients to stock. Bring to a boil. Reduce by half. Strain. In separate pan sweat extra shallot, garlic and wild mushrooms in clarified butter. When soft add stock and cream. Simmer for 3 minutes. Liquidize. Strain through fine sieve. Add truffle juice. Add cold butter in small pieces. Season.

NOTES ON INGREDIENTS

Many, if not most, of the recipes in this book call for luxurious ingredients or delicacies that may be hard to find or prohibitively expensive. The following list comments on many ingredients and where possible suggests alternatives. If there is no substitute, you may well be able to adapt the recipe to other ingredients. As mentioned before, the aim of this book is to fire the reader's imagination and to encourage experimentation. The only absolute requirements are that ingredients should be fresh and of prime quality so that your careful preparation and attention to detail will be repaid with first class results.

AQUAVIT Spirit (alcohol) flavored with caraway. Substitute: other caraway spirits, such as kümmel, but these are sweet. If this is undesirable, steep crushed caraway seeds in vodka.

ARTICHOKES French: *artichauts*. Large green thistle flowers. Soak in cold salted water to remove insects. To serve whole: cook in boiling water for about 25 minutes.

ARTICHOKE HEARTS trim away all leaves and hairy 'choke' in middle; cook in a blanc for 10 to 12 minutes. Available cooked in cans (French: *fonds d'artichauts*).

ARTICHOKES, JERUSALEM French: *topinambours*. Knobbly roots. Use in mousses and purées, cooked in a blanc until tender; or cook as potatoes. Peel, if desired, after cooking.

ASPARAGUS Wild asparagus has most flavor but difficult to obtain; next best is thin, fresh local asparagus. If using tips separately, save stalks for sauces and soups. Blanch tips for 2 minutes; stalks for 4 to 5 minutes.

AVOCADOS Hass avocados (with knobbly, blackish skin) have most flavor. Flesh discolors once cut: avoid by rubbing with lemon juice.

BACON For lardoons buy unsliced bacon. Blanch in unsalted water for 20 minutes. Cool. Cut into $\frac{1}{4}$ inch cubes. Fry.

BASIL Herb with smooth oval leaves; easy to grow indoors. Avoid dried basil. Preserve leaves by freezing with water in ice cubes, 3 or 4 to a cube.

BASIL BUTTER: butter flavored with finely chopped basil leaves. Added to dishes, the butter melts, distributing the flavor throughout. Can be done with most other herbs.

BASIL SAUCE (Italian: *pesto*): good for adding to sauces and salad dressing. 4c basil leaves/6 cloves garlic/2¾c Parmesan/⅔c pine nuts/olive oil. Blend dry ingredients in blender or food processor. Add oil to make a smooth purée.

BEANS, GREEN Choose smallest beans. Good in crudités, but blanch for 2 minutes first; 5 minutes for other uses.

BEEF Choose USDA Prime if possible. Finest cut is tenderloin, often sold as 'filet mignon' 'chateaubriaud', 'tournedos', 'medallions' or 'filet de boeuf'. Should have good marbling of fat. Trim away gristle. Remove 'chain' (gristly strip of meat) from side; save for casseroles, or hamburger.

BONE MARROW Butchers will generally chop up bones to make the marrow accessible. Use a spoon to scoop it out.

BROCCOLI Can be green, purple or yellow. Divide tips into clusters for decoration. Use stalks in purées, mousses and terrines. Blanch tips for 4 minutes, stalks for 8 to 10 minutes. Substitute: Cauliflower.

CABBAGE, SAVOY Crisp, green, wrinkled leaves good as wrappings for various fillings. Discard tough outer leaves. Detach other leaves. Blanch for 3 minutes. Trim off central rib. Fill. Substitutes: other cabbages, spinach, lettuce.

CARROTS Small 'finger' carrots have more delicate flavor. Don't peel, just brush gently under running tap, cut off ends; or for certain dishes retain top with 2 inches green stalk. Blanch whole carrots for 8 to 10 minutes. CARROT BALLS: use smallest parisienne cutter, blanch for 4 minutes. JULIENNE: blanch 1 to 2 minutes.

CAUL FAT French: *crépine*. Fatty covering of pig's intestines. Paper thin, translucent, with network of thicker strips. Use as wrapping for meats; fat melts and bastes the meat. No real substitute; but thinly sliced bacon could be used.

CAULIFLOWER Wash well in cold salted water to remove insects. Cut into small florets for decoration. Blanch for 2 to 4 minutes, according to size.

Substitute: broccoli.

CAVIAR Sevruga is best for hot dishes, Beluga for cold. Substitutes (not nearly as good but much less expensive): 'golden caviar' and salmon's eggs, from delicatessens; or, for decoration only, lumpfish roe which looks right but tastes very different from caviar, widely available.

CELERY ROOT Large root of a variety of celery. Nutty celery flavor. Grate raw for salads. Discolors when cut: avoid with lemon juice, or put in acidulated water (*page 155*). For purée: peel, slice and boil until tender.

CHAMPAGNE In sauces, substitute: dry sparkling wine.

CHANTERELLES See Mushrooms, wild.

CHERVIL Herb like delicate parsley; slight anise flavor. Not widely sold but easy to grow outdoors. Goes limp soon after cutting: revive by rinsing and shaking dry. Keeps for 2 to 3 days in vegetable compartment of refrigerator. Freeze as basil. Substitutes: parsley, fennel tops.

CHICKEN, BABY Normally known by French name: *poussin*. Choose fresh if possible; frozen have little taste. Save carcass for stock.

CHICKEN, SMOKED From delicatessens. Substitutes: smoked turkey or smoked ham.

CHIVES Small relative of onion. Stems have delicate oniony flavor, used as herb. Cut with scissors to avoid bruising. Purple flowers edible, make good decorations. Freeze as basil. Substitute: chopped scallion tops.

CILANTRO Fresh leaves of the coriander plant, also sold as 'Chinese parsley', resemble flat parsley but have powerful flavor: use sparingly. Sold by Mexican-American and Chinese shops, but easy to grow in sheltered spot. Freeze as basil. Substitute: parsley (but not coriander seed, which is a spice with quite different taste and uses).

CORAL See Scallops.

CRABS Choose large, live Dungeness or king crabs (markets usually cook crabs before selling them, so order a few days in advance). Cook for 15 minutes, or more if very large, in boiling bouillon with 1tsp salt per 1¼c. Let cool in liquid. Discard liquid, too salty for other use. Lever open shell. Discard gills and spongy parts, separate brown and white meat, pick out any shell splinters.

CRANBERRIES Red berries with astringent flavor. Used as decoration or made into sauce: almost cover with mixture of orange juice and water. Bring to a boil. Cook until berries start to pop. Add sugar (half the amount of berries), a touch of nutmeg and a few cloves. Keeps well in jars.

CROÛTONS Small circles or cubes of stale white bread without crusts, fried in oil until crisp and golden.

CUCUMBERS Keep in vegetable compartment of refrigerator. Salt slices to draw out juices which can make dishes watery. Wipe off salt after 30 minutes. Some people dislike the 'core' of immature seeds, which can be removed.
CUCUMBER BALLS: peel, form with parisienne cutter, blanch for 2 minutes.
CUCUMBER BARRELS: don't peel; cut into short lengths, remove 'core', trim into shapes like 'barrels', blanch for 3 minutes. Substitute: zucchini.

DANDELION LEAVES French: pissenlits. Slightly bitter taste, less so if very young or artificially bleached by being grown in cellars. Bleached leaves sold in some specialist shops. Pick wild leaves in spring only. Or grow your own outdoors and bleach them by putting a pot upside down over the plants. Substitute: curly endive.

DILL Feathery herb with anise flavor. Use seeds and leaves. Good with salmon and in salads; leaves used for decoration. Freeze as basil. Substitute: fennel tops.

DOUGH, PIE See Pastry.

DUCK MAGRET Breast of specially fattened ducks, available from delicatessens in vacuum packs. Firmer, meatier and tastier than ordinary duck breast; heavy layer of fat under skin. Grill, broil or fry with fat towards heat for 4 times as long as other side, to melt fat and crisp skin. Substitute: see next entry.

DUCKLING, LONG ISLAND Conventional name for common American type. Choose fresh if possible. Use breast as substitute for magret, legs for mousse.

EGGS Use at room temperature for best results. See also Quail's eggs.

ENDIVE Several types, including Belgian endive and radicchio (listed separately). All slightly bitter, good in salads. Curly endive (French: chicorée frisée), also known as chicory, has frizzy leaves, pale green with darker edges, crisp.

ENDIVE: also known as Batavian endive, escarole or chicory escarole, has broader leaves like romaine, sometimes with red tinged tips. Crisper than lettuce but more bitter.

ENDIVE, BELGIAN French: endive. Bleached shoots of a type of endive, also known as French endive or witloof. Slightly bitter, becoming more so when in contact with daylight. Good in salads. Discolors easily: keep wrapped in paper before use, wash, cut or tear up and serve quickly before it goes brown.

FIGS Green, black or purple. No special preparation, just wash. Substitutes: not canned or dried figs, which are quite different; use some other exotic fresh fruit.

FILO PASTRY See Pastry.

FIVE SPICE POWDER Chinese spice mixture (ng heung fun), consisting of anise, fennel seed, cloves, cinnamon and pepper, available from Chinese markets. Substitute: individual spices.

FOIE GRAS Fatted liver (normally of duck or goose). Use duck foie gras, cheaper than goose foie gras (though still very expensive) and with more flavor, in spite of being fattier. Not widely available, except in unsuitable pâté form. One liver weighs about 1lb. Soak in iced water to remove blood before cooking. Use a small knife to scrape away any traces of gall bladder (green patches) and cut out any veins. Excellent served hot. Substitutes: no real ones, but chicken liver or calf's liver can be prepared in same way.

GARLIC Peel cloves before use. Cut away any green center, which can be bitter and indigestible.

GELATIN If sheet gelatin is not available use powdered gelatin. Refer to package for equivalent measures and instructions on use, 3 sheets $= \frac{1}{2}$oz powdered gelatin.

GINGER Use fresh if possible. Peel and chop, slice or crush to develop its pungency. Substitutes: pickled ginger (soon geung or beni shoga, from Oriental shops), dried root or ground ginger.

GOOSE FAT Very rich flavor. From

specialist food stores. Substitutes: dripping or chicken fat.

GRAPEFRUIT White or pink. Peel and remove white pith. Cut between membranes to make skinless segments for garnish. Substitute: other citrus fruits.

GRAPES I like the French Muscat, beautifully sweet. To prepare: blanch in boiling water for 20 seconds, plunge into cold water, peel, halve, and remove seeds. Substitute: other larger grapes, though seedless ones are too small to make a good garnish.

KIDNEYS, CALF'S Quite expensive. Remove the surrounding fat (suet). Soak for 1 hour in milk to remove blood. Rinse, dry and cut in half lengthwise. Remove tough core. Slice or dice. Do not overcook; leave slightly pink. Substitute: see next entry.

KIDNEYS, LAMB'S Less expensive but excellent roasted pink in their suet. Roast about 10 minutes in a hot oven, trim off fat and slice thinly.

KOHLRABI Bulbous, mild flavored root of a variety of cabbage. Purple or green. Peel and use raw in crudités. Substitute: small turnips.

LAMB If you can, choose prime rib rack. One rack gives 4 portions. Use trimmings for minced lamb.

LAMB'S LETTUCE Also called field or corn salad. French: *mâche*. Small, oval salad leaves, grows wild. Rather sharp flavor. Wash well to remove sand.

LANGOSTINOS Also known as langoustines. Shellfish mainly imported from Chile, with mild, lobster-like flavor. Substitute: king prawns.

LARDOONS See Bacon.

LEEKS Where possible, use thin, young leeks. Cut into 1 inch lengths, wash well (often very dirty), and blanch for 4 minutes.
JULIENNE: use larger leeks. Substitutes: scallions or chives.

LEMONS Choose thin skinned lemons for segments or juice. A squeeze of lemon juice in sauces cuts down richness, balances saltiness. Also keeps cut surfaces of fruit from browning.

LIMES More subtle taste than lemons. Use segments quickly once cut, as they lose colour. Substitute: lemons.

LIVER, CALF'S Remove thin membrane from outside. Cook very quickly to sear outside but leave inside

pink. Substitute: lamb's liver.

LOBSTERS American lobsters from Maine, Nova Scotia or Newfoundland are best. Should be live. Cook as crabs, minimum 10 minutes, plus 5 minutes per extra lb. Separate head from tail and claws and remove meat. Use scissors to cut along each side of tail underbody. Remove meat in one piece. Split head, discard greyish sac, and use rest of head and shell for making stocks and sauces. Substitutes: spiny lobsters, langostinos or monkfish tails.

LYCHEES Fruit similar in texture to grapes. Peel off stiff shell and remove single stone. Substitute: canned lychees.

MELONS, CHARENTAIS Small, round; grayish yellow-green netted skin; orange flesh. Very sweet. Scent indicates ripeness. Substitute: cantaloupes.

MELONS, OGEN Small; green and yellow striped skin; pale green flesh. Very sweet. Scent indicates ripeness. Substitute: Galia melons.

MINT Several species of this herb: grow your favorite outdoors (in a pot, to avoid spreading). Use sparingly in salads and sauces. Freeze as basil.

MONKFISH Also known as angler or 'poor man's lobster'. Usually only fillets are sold. Dense, meaty texture; makes a substitute for the texture of lobster or scallops, but unfortunately not the flavor.

MULLET, RED Pink skinned fish. French nickname '*bécasse de mer*' (sea woodcock) because its liver is edible, as is the bird's. Remove scales, but leave skin on.

MUSSELS Best are blue mussels from October through April. Any that are open when bought and will not shut when nudged or tapped are dead: discard them. All should open when cooked: if any do not, discard these too.

MUSHROOMS, CULTIVATED Come in three forms; button, cups and flat. Flat have more flavor but produce more liquid when cooked.

MUSHROOMS, WILD Many recipes here specify wild mushrooms. Supermarkets now sometimes have a few kinds and often stock dried European ceps (see *right* for various names) and dried Chinese or Japanese mushrooms (usually *doong gwoe* or *shiitake*). In parts of the country you can gather your own. Use a good reference book; botanical names are given below. All except morels are autumn species. Substitutes: wild mushrooms of other species, often just as good; or cultivated mushrooms, which have little flavor in comparison, but which can be improved by adding some dried ceps.

CEPS (French: *cèpes*/German: *Steinpilze*/Italian: [*funghi*] *porcini*/botanical: *Boletus edulis* and other species): found in deciduous and coniferous woods. Brown, shiny cap (other species vary), spongy underside, thick stem. Strong flavor, especially when dried. Fresh: trim away sponge if soggy. Clean well to remove insects. Dried: soak until swollen. Rinse well.

CHANTERELLES (French: *girolles*/botanical: *Cantharellus cibarius*): found in deciduous woods. Trumpet shape, bright yellow. Occasionally on sale dried. Particularly good in sauces. Do not overcome or their chewy texture becomes tough.

HORNS OF PLENTY (French: *trompettes des morts*/botanical: *Cratellerus cornucopoides*): found under beech trees. Little, almost black trumpets prized more for their color than their faint flavor. Sometimes used to fake diced truffle in pâtés.

MORELS (French: *morilles*/botanical: *Morchella esculenta* and other species): found in woods and fields in spring. Cap looks like conical brown sponge, with large holes all over. Delicious, but one of the most expensive fungi to buy. Shape makes them good for stuffing. May be bought canned or dried. Fresh or dried: rinse very well to remove grit.

OYSTER MUSHROOMS (French: *pleurotes*/botanical: *Pleurotus ostreatus*): stemless 'bracket' fungus growing on dying deciduous trees. Gray cap with whitish gills, meaty flavor, edible only when young.

WOOD HEDGEHOG MUSHROOMS (French: *pieds de mouton*/botanical: *Hydnum repandum*): found in deciduous woods. Yellowy brown with 'rubber brush' spines insted of gills, needing careful cleaning. Solid, good flavor.

NASTURTIUM Garden flower with edible leaves, flowers and seeds. Leaves taste peppery (like watercress, a related plant); good in salads. Flowers make edible decoration. (Seeds formerly used

as substitute for capers.)

NETTLES Pick young stinging nettle leaves (wear gloves). Avoid flowering plants. Discard stems. Nettles are not on sale. Substitutes: spinach or sorrel.

NUTMEG Spice useful for seasoning both savory and sweet dishes. Buy whole nutmegs and grate as needed.

OILS OLIVE OIL: use first pressing 'extra virgin' oil where its strong flavor is an advantage: and where this is unwanted, rather than inferior olive oil use a refined, deodorized type such as:
PEANUT OIL French: *huile d'arachide*.
SESAME OIL: nutty flavor. Becoming more widely available. Substitute: mixture of peanut oil and tahina (sesame paste, from Middle Eastern or health food shops).
WALNUT OIL (French: *huile de noix*) and HAZELNUT OIL (French: *huile de noisettes*) are not widely sold and are expensive, but give excellent nutty flavor in cold and warm salad dressings. Keep refrigerated once opened.

OYSTERS No longer true that these are only edible during months containing the letter R; different kinds are available all year round. Open with special oyster knife. Reserve juice for sauce or poaching liquid. Poach for 30 seconds.

PARTRIDGE Small game bird with pale flesh. Substitutes: any small game bird or guinea fowl.

PASTRY FILO: buy ready made from larger stores and Greek shops. Dries out quickly once opened. Keep well wrapped. Work quickly. Brush each sheet lightly with melted butter. See diagrams on *page 138*.
PUFF PASTRY AND PIE DOUGH: easier to make than filo, but ready-made types are widely available and are usually good.

PEARS I prefer Bartlett pears for eating fresh, but choose Comice for poached savory pear dishes. To $2\frac{1}{2}$ qt water add: juice of 2 lemons/1 bay leaf/ 2 cloves/1 stick cinnamon.

PEPPER, CAYENNE Very hot, orange powder made from chilli peppers: use carefully.

PEPPERCORNS Black, white and green. Use freshly ground black where distinctive peppery taste is required and black specks don't matter. White are hot but less pungent; use in creamy sauces. Green, available canned in brine, are a 'nouvelle cousine' speciality which I consider overrated. (Pink peppercorns, from a different plant, were a passing fad; now known to be actually poisonous if consumed in large quantities.)

PEPPERS, SWEET BELL Also called capsicums or pimientos. Green, red, yellow and other colors. Must be firm and shiny; avoid soft or wrinkled ones. Deep fry, broil, grill or put in hot oven until skin blisters. Peel, halve and seed.

PESTO See under Basil.

PIGEONS Where possible choose corn fed pigeons, tender though expensive. Roasted pink, thinly sliced breasts attractive in salads. Substitute: quails.

QUAILS Small birds now raised commercially and even sold ready boned in some places. Others may bone them if asked. Substitutes: any small game birds or 'baby chickens' poussins).

QUAIL'S EGGS Tiny eggs taste exactly like hen's eggs; however, their size is a novelty. Substitute: smallest available hen's eggs.

RADICCHIO Usual Italian name for red salad leaf also called 'red lettuce' (actually it's an endive). Bitter, but good used sparingly in salads where it looks most striking. Substitute for flavor only: Belgian endive.

RADISHES, WHITE ORIENTAL French: crosnes. Small spiral tuber good eaten raw. Sometimes sold as loh baak in Chinese or daikon in Japanese markets. Wash well; no need to peel. Substitute: small turnips.

RASPBERRIES Don't wash; it spoils them. Pick over for moldy fruit and insects. Frozen raspberries are good for sauces.

RAVIOLI If making it yourself, roll out the pasta very thinly. Can be filled with almost anything you fancy. Ready-made fresh ravioli, now widely sold, is usually excellent.

ROQUEFORT Sharp blue cheese. Nearest substitutes: Pipo Crème and Stilton, but both lack its bite.

SAFFRON Spice made from crocus stamens. Bright yellow color, unique flavor. Very expensive. If stamens are bought, soak in a little warm water before using them. Substitute for color only: turmeric.

SALMON Use wild king salmon if possible. Farmed salmon can be used but have less flavor and lack firmness. Ask fishmonger for fillets rather than steaks. Substitute: salmon trout.

SCALLOPS Open shell with special knife. Remove sandy sac and rinse well to remove grit. Orange roe, known as coral, delicious used whole, puréed or made into mousse. Scallops and coral can be marinated in seasoned lime or lemon juice and eaten raw. Substitute: monkfish has similar texture, but nothing can duplicate flavor.

SEA BASS One of the best saltwater fish, with a meaty texture. Expensive. Substitute: any firm fleshed white fish.

SEA URCHINS Also known as sea egg. Spiky, spherical shell contains edible orange roe. Seldom sold except at specialist fishmongers. Ensure loose spines have been removed from inside. Cut flattish top off shell with scissors or special urchin cutter. Drain. Filter juice with sieve, and use in recipe with roes. Rinse shell to use as decorative container.

SEAWEED Type sold by fishmongers as garnish for oysters is not edible (though other kinds are). Blanch for 30 seconds till brilliant green, but not longer or it starts to pop and goes gluey.

SHALLOT Small, brown, elongated relative of onion with smoother flavor. Peel and chop very finely for sauces.

SNOW PEAS Also called podded peas, sugar peas, mangetouts and Chinese pea pods. Snap off the ends. Blanch for 1 minute. Reheat in slightly sweetened water, or sprinkle with a little sugar. In crudités: blanch for 30 seconds.

SOLE Use English when affordable. Skin both sides, black and white. Remove 4 fillets. Use bones for stock. Substitute: lemon sole (a kind of dab, not nearly as good).

SPINACH Wash very thoroughly. To use leaves as wrapping: blanch for 30 seconds, dry and trim off central rib.

SWEETBREADS Calf's sweetbreads are best. Soak in iced salted water to extract blood. Cook whole in unsalted boiling water for 10 minutes. Leave to cool in liquid. Remove and weight between two plates overnight. Remove gristly parts and as much of the outside film as you can without the sweetbreads falling apart. Slice or dice. Substitute: lamb's sweetbreads.

THYME Several varieties of this herb, all easy to grow outdoors. Strong flavor. Use tips and small stems, chopped or whole (remove before serving) in stocks and sauces. If old and woody, strip leaves and discard stems. Dries well, or freeze as basil.

TOMATOES To peel: blanch for 10 seconds to loosen skin. If necessary, start peeling by inserting knife tip.

TOMATOES, CHERRY Tiny, sweet, good for garnishing. Peel as ordinary tomatoes. Use whole or halved.

TRUFFLES Best kinds black French and white Alba (Italian); others markedly inferior. Use only the best, though appallingly expensive, very sparingly. Peel, save peelings and chop for sauces. Fresh are best but good quality canned available: choose top grade 'primeur cuisson'. Peelings and juice can also be bought in cans. Substitute: 'garnishing paste' in cans is a poor quality alternative without any flavor.

TURBOT Large flat fish, expensive. Fillet, reserve bones for stock. Skin. Substitute: brill.

TURMERIC Powdered spice used as color substitute for saffron, but flavor is quite different.

TURNIPS Very small, young turnips are good raw in crudités. Peel. Turnip balls make good garnish. Use smallest parisienne cutter. Blanch for 3 minutes.

VEAL Use white milk fed veal tenderloin: not cheap but very little waste. Substitutes: veal sirloin, or beef tenderloin or lamb sirloin.

VINEGARS Flavored vinegars can now be bought in many shops. If unavailable, use white or red wine vinegar.

WATERCRESS Wash very well to remove small slugs or snails. Blanch for 20 seconds.

WOODCOCK Small, delicate game bird. Should not be allowed to become too high. Cooked and served undrawn: liver and other entrails considered a delicacy (but gizzard must be discarded). Substitutes: quail or snipe.

ZUCCHINI French: *courgette*. Choose the smallest you can find. Blanch for 3 to 6 minutes according to size. For recipes using flowers, substitute spinach or lettuce leaves to enclose mousse.

GLOSSARY OF COOKING TECHNIQUES AND EQUIPMENT

ACIDULATED WATER Water with a little vinegar or lemon juice added. Used to cover cut fruits or vegetables to prevent browning, and for poaching eggs to stop the white from spreading.

BAIN-MARIE Used for very gentle cooking of delicate foods and sauces. Food is put in a container above or in a pan of warm water, and so heated indirectly. The same can be done in an oven by standing a dish in a pan of water, which protects from the intensity of direct heat.

BASTE To spoon fat or cooking liquids over foods during cooking in order to keep them moist.

BLANC Mixture used to preserve color of white or pale vegetables during cooking. Mix 3 Tbsp flour with 3 Tbsp water. Add to 5c water. Mix well. Pass through fine sieve. Season. Add juice of 1 lemon and $\frac{3}{4}$ stick (6 Tbsp) unsalted butter.

BLANCH To cook vegetables for a short time in boiling water or a blanc. Purpose may be to remove bitterness; to soften slightly; to loosen skins for peeling; and to intensify color. Blanching times are given wherever appropriate. Use large pan with plenty of salted water (or blanc). Bring to a boil. Add vegetables. Leave pan uncovered. Bring back to a boil: time from this moment. When time is up, remove vegetables and at once plunge them into bowl of iced water to arrest cooking.

BLENDER See Food processor.

CLARIFY To clear of solids or impurities. Clarified butter resists burning at high temperatures. Melt butter gently. Leave to stand for a few minutes. Pour slowly through fine muslin, leaving sediment in pan. Keeps very well in the refrigerator.

COURT-BOUILLON Cooking water flavored, as by adding stock.

DEGLAZE To add a liquid to a pan after frying or roasting to loosen the tasty residue. The mixture can then be used as basis for a sauce.

DICE To cut into small cubes.

EMULSIFY To form an emulsion, the blending of an oily with a watery liquid.

Milk is a natural emulsion; mayonnaise is one you make. Emulsions are unstable and liable to separate.

FLATTEN To beat a fillet of fish or meat with a mallet until extremely thin. It can then be shaped into an envelope or container for filling.

FOLD To combine delicate ingredients such as whipped cream or egg whites, where stirring or beating would destroy the foam. Use a large metal spoon. Lift one substance and turn it gently over the other, repeating until the two are more or less mixed; blending totally would also destroy the delicate structure of the foam.

FOOD PROCESSOR AND BLENDER Most of the recipes in this book allow the use of either machine. Sometimes a food processor gives a slightly lumpy result. If so, pass the food through a sieve.

JULIENNE To cut into fine strips; the result is also called a julienne.

LARD To thread a strip of an ingredient through meat or fish. Larding needles are sold for the purpose. Generally larding is done with strips of fat, to moisten food; but in this book it is done with truffle and salmon strips for decorative effect.

MARINATE To soak meat or fish in a marinade, a liquid mixture that moistens and flavors it. Marinades containing acid ingredients such as vinegar or lemon juice, or certain fresh fruit juices which contain natural enzymes, tenderize meat and act on fish in the same way as cooking.

MEDALLION Small circular slice.

PARISIENNE CUTTER Scoop for making balls of fruits or vegatables. Sometimes called a melon baller. There are various sizes.

PIPE To force a mixture through the nozzle of a forcing bag. Done to create decorative effects, often using a fancy nozzle; or to fill hollow items.

POACH To cook gently in simmering water, acidulated water or court-bouillon. Soft-poached eggs: tip out of shells directly into acidulated water. Cook until white hardens but yolk remains soft. Remove with slotted spoon. Plunge directly into iced water to arrest cooking. The fresher the eggs, the better the results.

REDUCE To boil a liquid to evaporate the water content, concentrating flavor and consistency.

SAUTÉ To cook in a shallow pan with butter or oil over a fast heat. This seals the outside of the food, thereby retaining the juices inside.

SEED To remove seeds. Usually done to improve presentation rather than flavor; but it makes tomatoes less watery.

SKIN To remove skin. Often done for appearance only. However, skins of tomatoes and some other vegetables may be indigestible and bitter, and are best removed. Instructions are given where appropriate.

STEAM To cook above a boiling or simmering liquid, in a steamer or bain-marie. The top section of the pan must be well fitting and covered to keep the steam in.

SWEAT To cook over a low heat, usually in butter or oil, causing juices to run out of food and soften it. Salt may be added to help extract the liquid.

INDEX

Main references are
given first in roman type.
Italic numerals indicate
recipes in which the item
appears.